P

MW00639194

"A brilliant take on how to design your own creative community! This is a must-read for any emerging leader."

— ERIN KRAMPETZ BOYD

Co-Founder of **Ashoka U** and Business Operations for **Culdesac**, which is building the first car-free neighborhood in the U.S.

"An essential read for anyone in community and economic development professions, or anyone that just wants to make a positive contribution to their community. Spud weaves captivating and highly entertaining stories about success, failure, and overcoming adversity from his own creative practice in dozens of communities, providing powerful tools for creative transformation with humor, humility, and honest self-reflection. This book is hugely relatable and difficult to put down; it is one influential guide that I will be recommending widely to colleagues and communities alike."

— MICHAEL FORTUNATO

Founding Partner of **Creative Insight Community Development**

"Spud is hands down the most creative community builder I've ever met! In his book, he showcases his unique journey step-by-step, the highs and lows he navigated along the way, and how you too can shape the community of your dreams."

— ALEXIS TAYLOR

World Economic Forum Global Shaper and Davos Lab Taskforce Co-Chair

"Spud is what would happen if you took the imagination and creativity of a second grader and paired it with the wisdom of a 90-year-old professor. It is a gift to meet someone with this level of creativity and skill to effectively bring these dreams to life. This book is a terrific read!"

— DUSTIN LIU

United Nations, U.S. Youth Observer

DESIGNING
CREATIVE
COMMUNITIES

DESIGNING
CREATIVE
COMMUNITIES

YOUR TOWN IS YOUR CANVAS.
LEARN HOW TO **MAKE YOUR MARK**

SPUD MARSHALL

my creative community

ISBN   978-1-7376389-0-2   *Paperback*
        978-1-7376389-1-9   *Ebook*
        978-1-7376389-2-6   *Audiobook*

Edited by Michael Schroeder
Copyediting by Adam Greenberg
Cover art by Spud Marshall
Interior layout by Victoria Dickson

www.mycreative.community

To the sometimes overlooked
who dream of brighter futures and
dare to invite the rest of us along.

This one's for you.

TABLE OF CONTENTS

INTRODUCTION

DESIGNING CREATIVE COMMUNITIES

I FOUND WHAT I NEEDED to bring my best idea to life in a dumpster.

If you were passing by on the street, you would have seen only my legs sticking out as I tossed trash excitedly to the side. This was the fourth dumpster I had been in that evening, and I'd learned over the last two weeks to go at night to limit the stares.

Dumpsters are not where people typically go looking for inspiration. But beyond the grime and overpowering smell, I knew this was exactly where I'd find what I needed. Of course, I made sure not to tell the mayor that I dug through the trash to find it. I simply wanted to show her how we could make our town a better place to call home.

————

You and I may not share a love for dumpster diving, but I suspect that we share a love for wanting to make our communities better places. We want them to be places that are full of life, possibility, and engagement.

There's likely things about your town that you love, and aspects that you wished were different. But often, we feel stuck not knowing how to tangibly contribute to making a change. You might wonder which ideas are worth pursuing, and what it would take to make them a reality. You may also be unsure if you're the right person to make the changes you want to see.

This book is the story of how some of the best ideas for designing creative communities emerge from unsuspecting places, like dumpsters. Whether you are new to community building or have been at this work for years, we'll walk through how you can uncover and pursue creative ideas in your town.

You'll discover that you don't have to be the mayor of your city or even a community leader to change where you live for the better. You just have to be deeply curious and persistently proactive.

You don't need to worry about whether you are creative enough either. You simply need to be willing to venture into the nooks and crannies of our world, because the best ideas are often waiting for everyday people – like you and me – to stumble upon them. It takes being inquisitive, having an open mind, and getting out into your community.

What I want to do is give you the tools to develop your ideas and run with them so you can transform your community into a thriving, equitable, hopeful, and creative place – and have a lot of fun along the way.

But before we forge ahead, let me provide some context for you as to how I got my start in community building.

In my mid-20s, I had few reasons to dream small. I was living in State College, Pennsylvania, blazing my own path, much to the confusion of my parents. A few years prior, I had finished my undergrad degree in mechanical engineering, a major that often leads to a well-defined career path and stable income. But I graduated in the middle of a recession in 2008, and my well-orchestrated plans quickly fell apart.

You don't always see opportunities for what they are in the moment. For me, the employment crisis helped pave an alternate career path. My original plan was to become an Imagineer for Disney. I imagined I'd design fog machine cannons for pirate ships and learn how to carve fake rocks (a goal I still hold for myself to this day). But with that career path no longer an immediate option, I decided to apply my creative energy to where I lived instead.

State College is a gem of a town. Roughly 50,000 full-time residents and just as many college students call our Happy Valley in central Pennsylvania home. Nestled between rolling mountains, our town has consistently been ranked as one of the top U.S. towns for outdoor adventure. It's been named among the safest places to raise a family, and one of the smartest regions in the country, based on the number of people who have PhDs here. (It's an imperfect metric, to be sure, but however you measure it, we have a lot of brainpower in this community.)

State College has also gotten high marks for being one of the most bikeable towns in the country, and Penn State has been recognized as one of the most accepting universities for the LGBTQ+ community. There's so much to love about this place.

But there are also a lot of things that frustrated me while studying here as a student. Divisions exist in the community that you might not recognize unless you lived here. A few families exert significant influence on what happens in State College, and old guard thinking has kept many innovations from seeing the light of day. Despite having a vibrant international student body, the town is predominantly white, with plenty of room for advancing equity and racial justice. Young people flock here to study, but usually leave as soon as they graduate. I've met very few young professionals who survived their 20s in State College – something I now consider to be a badge of honor and resume builder.

The town was just the right size for me to make my mark without getting lost in the crowd, as I might have in a larger city. Without a clear career path or even a job title for what I hoped to pursue, I made it my goal to call State College my place of work. In many ways, I hoped this would be my canvas. I just wasn't sure what I'd create.

My mechanical engineering training taught me to view places as problems to be solved – as an intricate web of sewer pipes, bridges, and traffic lights. But in visiting Disney as a child, I learned to see places as a life-size canvas. I was fascinated with the possibility of interacting with State College through the same lens of wonder and imagination.

As I set my creative sights on State College, my friends were gracious enough to let me sleep on their couches. Most of them had steady jobs and life plans well sketched out. I imagine they were as confused about what I was doing as my parents were. But they seemed curious to see what would happen if they took a bet on that one friend with a crazy idea.

For a whole year, I couch-surfed and worked alongside some of my closest childhood friends. In high school, we'd made a pact after graduation to work together to change the world for the better. I still remember the moment. We were standing under a basketball hoop in my friend's driveway when we naively shook on it. Those same friends would become some of my closest collaborators and business partners.

We had big dreams for improving our town, but no idea how to do that. In those early days, we didn't have the mayor's personal cell phone number or hang out with philanthropists, investors, or real estate developers. Maybe you're in a similar place: You want to create change but aren't sure where to start.

Our journey taught us the very thing our town needed was a place for people to take that first step. We needed a space where people could drop in, share an idea, meet a collaborator, and begin acting on their vision for a better town. We envisioned a creative lab where people could turn over a new leaf and try something innovative.

In many ways, that's where my improvised career path really started to take shape, and where a pact turned into a venture. With nothing more to our business plan, we bought a web domain, started a nonprofit, and went to work finding a space for our new organization, which we called New Leaf.

When you don't have any money, connections, or experience, you start with what you know, and we knew craigslist. Every day I would scan the latest posts, scrolling through offers of well-worn, cat-scratched recliners and heaping piles of scrap metal and railroad ties. We love a good yard sale in central Pennsylvania, and scouring craigslist for bargains is the digital equivalent of going house to house to hunt for bargains.

Eventually, we found a professional photographer who was renting out his basement storage closet. There was no price listed – likely because he didn't think it would be of much value to anyone – so when we reached out and asked what the rent was, we caught him off-guard. He turned the question around and asked us how much we wanted to pay.

We made up a number on the fly. "How does $300 a month sound?"

He quickly agreed.

We had learned our first lesson in negotiation: Always start low! Our photographer friend would have been OK with $50. But we didn't know better at the time. So with no donors, grants, or fundraising plans, we had our first expense. We needed to raise $300 each month. Fortunately, one of our friends held an actual job and was generous enough to pay the rent, while the rest of us donated our time. It seemed like a fair trade.

I soon found myself living out of this storage closet that we'd converted into an office 18 hours a day while spending the remaining few hours sleeping on friends' couches. We hung up inspirational quotes on the walls, designed our own swag to sell, and began teaching ourselves how to build a website. With no budget for advertising or promotion, we used chalk to draw big arrows on the sidewalk that pointed to our space. When that didn't work, we moved our desks onto the sidewalk to interact with passersby. We spent months getting the space ready to unveil to the community.

Then catastrophe struck. I'm still not sure if it was a crack in the pipes or a backed-up drain that was to blame for soiling our dream.

But whatever the cause, sewer water flowed freely underneath the walls into our newly painted office.

It was coming from the bathroom located in the photographers' office – which was locked. We were simply in his adjacent storage closet, so we had no way to turn off the water. With no access to the source of the chaos, my friend and I watched helplessly as our craigslist furniture decreased in what little value they initially once held.

Regrettably, we didn't have the photographer's number, but we could see where water was streaming in from underneath the drywall. With little time to react, my friend hoisted me up into the drop ceiling. I climbed precariously above the panels, hoping that the loosely strung-up metal frame would hold my weight as I inched forward above the photographer's office. I went back and forth in my head between imagining I was either pulling off a great bank robbery or preparing for an epic belly flop into liquid manure. Fortunately, the scenario that played out was more like the bank heist. I lowered myself onto the toilet and put all of my mechanical engineering training to good use to turn off the waterline. Four years of college education validated. I'd stopped the poop water. But the damage was done, and so was our office.

A few weeks later, we moved down the block to basement space No. 2. And with the plumbing drama behind us, we began to dream up our grand plan to pitch to the mayor.

———

It took a while before we could call the mayor a friend, but our efforts seemed to be attracting attention. At the same time, people weren't quite sure what we were doing, primarily because we were still figuring that out ourselves. We didn't have a mission statement, a defined budget, or an organizational structure.

We were making it up as we went. There was a thrill in discovering how to build an organization from nothing that kept my friends and I going through many long nights. We even loved mundane challenges, like navigating the IRS system while filing our taxes and applying for nonprofit status.

We embraced the joys of not "working for the man" and being able to operate on our own timeline. Of course, that turned out to be 12-plus hours most days with neither benefits nor security. No one tells you that the man actually has things to offer. Still, despite the long hours, we were entirely invested in building something of our own.

In practice, what we offered our community was quite simple. If someone walked into our space and shared their latest dream, we would print it out, frame it, and hang it on a white wall. People shared all kinds of ideas for what we could do in the community. Those ranged from installing vertical hydroponic growing systems to establishing an environmental bill of rights to using lunar panels to harness the sun's energy via the moon. Nothing was off-limits. As ideas evolved, teams would form to define concrete goals. As momentum grew around each idea, we would move the frames to our orange wall: the project wall.

That was it. That was what we did. We helped turn ideas into projects.

Eventually, as we honed this skill, we could more easily get an audience with influential people in town. The mayor was near the top of our list.

After spending 18 months in our second office space – 300

square feet underground, with lots of pipes in the ceiling overhead that served as an uneasy reminder of our early days – we began to dream about expansion.

This is typical of most ideas. You start thinking about how to scale an idea itself rather than the anticipated impact of the idea. We didn't know exactly what kind of impact we hoped to have. We just knew that we needed more space on our walls to hang frames. It took me a while to realize that an idea and the impact it has are two different things. You can grow your impact without needing to scale the idea into something bigger.

But we were young, dumb, and naive. So in our minds, bigger was better. We figured what we really needed was more wall space.

We asked to meet with the mayor to discuss plans for how we might launch a co-working and innovation hub for our town. We envisioned a thriving community space. This would be a place where new ideas could flourish, freelancers could work, and events could be held. We photoshopped a picture of our office with multiple versions of ourselves to playfully illustrate how cramped the space was and make our pitch for an expanded venue. It worked, and eventually, the mayor agreed to meet with us.

We were excited to be invited to her office on the municipal building's top floor to share our vision. Sadly, at the time, about the only reason I could think of that people would go to this building was to pay a parking ticket. I know others shared that narrow perception as well. It certainly didn't seem like a place where you'd go to hang out and casually exchange ideas.

The council chamber was an intimidating room where people with more power sat above you and used words like "whereas" and "presiding." I imagined they wore white wigs and all had British accents. Thick glass stood between the public and police and parking departments – not a particularly warm or engaging setup. And the hallways were painted a drab tan, featuring outdated photos of our town 100 years ago.

When I thought of our thriving community – this building was far from what I envisioned.

So as we entered our meeting with the mayor – on the top floor of this fortress – it felt like we were approaching nobility in a castle rather than meeting an old friend. The building was supposed to be a welcoming space for people in the community, but it didn't feel that way to us.

As we walked up the stairs to the mayor's office, we glanced into a large vacant room at the end of a hallway that was littered with boxes and other odds and ends. It was an open space with huge windows overlooking the entire downtown. The walls were exposed with insulation and wires hung precariously from the ceiling, but it had serious potential. Our curiosity had been sparked.

My friends and I looked at each other with a knowing grin. We immediately began to envision this space as the future home of New Leaf. We could see it clear as day.

But we weren't ready to pitch that vision to the mayor. So we told her instead about our general plan for launching a community innovation hub somewhere in town. She nodded and smiled. We were young, and it was never easy to determine whether someone was doing us a favor by offering their time or genuinely interested in supporting us. So we didn't tell her about our dumpster diving plan. We only shared a half-truth.

If there was one thing we discovered running our own organization fresh out of college, it was that we had to show someone our vision, not just tell them about it. We were never taught that nuance years before in kindergarten.

When you have influence and power, people listen to your words. But when you don't have that kind of sway and authority, you need to do more than talk about your idea. For those wanting to reshape their communities, that means giving neighbors something they can touch and tangibly connect with while providing them with an experience they will remember.

We had talked with countless people around town over the past two years and were often shuffled on to the next important person. But in the moments where we had got traction on an idea, it was always because we dove headlong into building something that the community could tangibly see.

Keeping that in mind, we ended our conversation with the mayor by making an innocent offer.

We told her that we noticed the room at the end of the hallway needed to be organized. "If you let us into the space for 24 hours, we would happily come in and clean it up for you."

It's hard for anyone, especially a mayor, to turn down free help. She said yes, and we agreed to a date a few weeks in the future. It wasn't actually that we needed that much time to recruit volunteers. We had volunteers. We needed the lead time to raid dumpsters.

We planned to spend the first four hours cleaning up the space as promised. After that, we conveniently failed to mention that we would use the remaining 20 hours to transform the space into a life-size, cardboard mock-up of our vision for a community innovation hub.

Of course, when you're on a shoestring budget, you have to think creatively about where you get your materials. And the best place to find good, cheap (i.e., free) cardboard is a dumpster.

So for the next few weeks, we spent every night dumpster diving, collecting as much cardboard as we could. With what little money we had, we bought dozens of rolls of colored duct tape. Then we spent all of our remaining waking hours building our cardboard mock-up.

We built cardboard desks, cardboard chairs, cardboard cut-outs of people and cardboard plants and pictures to decorate the space. We made a fancy new sign out of cardboard and color-coded everything with duct tape. Orange represented the co-working desks, blue tape was used to trace the open space we'd set aside for events, and we applied green tape to outline where the private meeting rooms were located. Cardboard silhouettes lounged around our office on the same couches I slept on. Our tiny 300-square-foot basement office was overflowing with cardboard scenery. It was like a poorly financed prop shop for a low-budget movie.

We hoped the mayor wouldn't catch on, and we began to spread the word that there would be a grand launch party for a mysterious new space – the entire community was encouraged to join us. Targeted curiosity is often the best way to rally support when building something new.

The day came. We cleaned up as promised, and then spent hours hanging our cardboard village from the rafters. As the event approached, we stared out the windows at the street below and wondered if anyone would show up. Would the mayor be mad?

To our surprise, the town showed up en masse. The mayor came as well. She was smiling, and unlike in pitch meetings, where a cordial reception doesn't always lead to a partnership, we could tell she was thrilled with the idea.

The night was a huge achievement. Hundreds of community members streamed in throughout the evening. People were networking, laughing, and dreaming about how they could contribute to our town as well. Other politicians, entrepreneurs, and philanthropists joined us. We hosted professors and met with parents while their kids played. In a town plagued by silos, this night represented something new: a chance for members of our community to collaborate in ways that they hadn't realized was possible.

We spend so much time getting frustrated with how our towns typically operate. We complain about what we don't like or point to other towns that are doing it better. We get trapped in unhelpful narratives of how things used to be, which plagues our ability to see how they could be.

During our cardboard launch party, folks walked down the hallway past the photos of our town 100 years prior. Then they turned the corner and came into a previously vacant storage closet, where they got a glimpse of what our town could look like 100 years in the future. That's the very essence of community building: creating moments of wonder. These are moments of possibility, creative collaboration, and radical re-imagining.

———————

Most of the evening was a blur as I bounced around, meeting with collaborators and others we planned to work with in the future. But for one brief moment, I remember climbing up a few rungs of a ladder in the corner of the room. I looked out over the crowd and I was struck by what we had created.

Too often, we think about our communities only in terms of what we get from them. But the same sentiment JFK espoused decades ago – in asking us to think not only about what our country does for us but what we can do for our country – applies to our local communities as well. These are not only places where we live, work, learn, and play; they are places where we are meant to meaningfully contribute.

Our cities and towns serve as more than the backdrop for big moments in our lives, like where we went to school, fell in love, or found our first job. They aren't just shaped by the wealthy and powerful and the politicians, either. We all have a stake, and we all have something to contribute. As each guest walked into our cardboard village, we gave them a simple prompt: to add to the emerging story of State College.

Nothing was polished, and there was no elaborate PowerPoint presentation. We didn't have fancy tablecloths or assigned seating. We just managed to scrape by feeding our guests with a veggie tray we picked up from the grocery store that morning. Our entire space was made of nothing more than cardboard and duct tape. Yet by lowering the barriers, our vision became accessible. Everyone began to think about how they could contribute to our community.

You may feel intimidated not knowing how to contribute to your town. Maybe you've sat through a presentation from a consultant or politician analyzing your community, but left without knowing where you fit in or what you could do. Or perhaps you have the start of an idea and are waiting to find a collaborator. Maybe you see cool things happening in other towns when you travel and wish you could help make that a reality in yours. Often we stop short of acting because we think we must have it all figured out first. We assume we need formal plans and strategies and funding and partners.

But you don't. You don't need degrees, training, a fancy PowerPoint presentation to lay out your vision, or even cash. You just need your voice, plus a healthy sprinkling of creative persistence.

As folks entered the room that night where we laid out our vision for a community innovation hub, we encouraged them to add to it.

Add your ideas.

Add your design suggestions.

Add your business cards and connections.

Add your hopes and concerns and dreams.

Add your vision for what constitutes an amazing place to call home.

Rarely are we given permission to add to our communities in such tangible ways and such a playful manner.

If you're like me, you grew up believing that organizations, companies and communities are primarily shaped from the top-down. The subtle message is that people in power influence the way things are, and the rest of us fill in the cracks of the hierarchy.

Our cardboard village proposed that the opposite can be true. This was a bottom-up revolution. This was a chance for everyone's voice to be heard in the design of their community. And that made all the difference.

THE CANVAS
FRAMEWORK

WITHIN ONE YEAR OF OUR cardboard mock-up, we received $100,000 to renovate and build our community innovation hub in that very space. There was a grand ribbon-cutting with really important people posing for photo-ops. The mayor was there, along with the press. But there were also lots of regular people – people like you and me – hanging out and proud of what we had built together. Our $200 duct tape and cardboard bet resulted in an investment of 500 times that amount and a pretty awesome community space.

A decade after the cardboard village experiment, I've been fortunate to look back on having led multiple community spaces and social ventures in my town that contribute to the "live, work, learn, play" pillars of a thriving community.

THRIVING
CREATIVE COMMUNITIES

Elements of a thriving creative community.

Creative communities emerge through unique living spaces, collaborative work locations, experiential learning opportunities, and inclusive moments to play. Polling from Americans for the Arts found that 72% of people believe the arts unify a community regardless of age, race, or ethnicity. And collectively, arts and cultural efforts contribute more to the nation's economy than tourism or agriculture. Creativity is central to the well-being of our communities.

After starting New Leaf, our town's first collaboration and co-working hub, I launched the co.space. We purchased and transformed a large boarding home into a residential co-living space for 20 young changemakers to live together year-round. Our goal was to retain creative young professionals in our region, and we'd discovered that getting them plugged into a meaningful community was frequently more of a driver to stay than seeking a particular job. The house has sparked many relationships, from new business partners to even once-strangers getting married, and has taught me about the nuance and magic of fostering community and how so many of us crave deep relationships.

A few years later, I launched a third space: 3 Dots. Designed as a downtown arts and innovation event center, the space has become a hub for our region's creative talent. Our goal has been to amplify our town's culture and help people connect to local opportunities for creative changemaking. Creativity emerges from the spontaneous collision of new ideas, thought, and practice. Our space was designed to increase the number of those collisions in town by facilitating a third space between work and home.

While launching these ventures, I worked extensively on education efforts – from universities and colleges to self-directed learning programs and K-12 schools – to ensure that our communities were places where people could learn and grow. I incorporated self-directed apprenticeships into my ventures and ran more than 50 immersive retreats for students dedicated to creative changemaking.

These organizations and efforts have collectively brought in over $1 million in grants and investment capital, engaged tens of thousands of people, and converted more than 10,000 square feet into thriving community spaces. They have allowed members of our community to become active builders of our future and spun off countless side projects and initiatives thanks to the collaboration that takes place there. Some have built thriving food hubs to support our local growers, farmers, and restaurants. Others have built supportive and inclusive dance communities out of our spaces.

The irony is that very few of the people leading these sub-communities would call themselves community builders. They would use terms like scientist or entrepreneur, farmer or artist, dancer or student. Community building isn't a career path or job title for most of us. It's often not a label people ever use to describe themselves or what they're doing, even as they make meaningful contributions that help develop and shape their communities.

If you've picked up this book, my guess is you care about making your town a thriving community as well. You may not call yourself a community builder either, and that's OK. I'm less interested in labels and buzzwords for how we describe the work. I simply care about helping people design creative communities in their own unique way. You can call yourself a collaboration catalyst or an ecosystem engineer, or not refer to community building in any formal way at all.

But because so few people know how to label this work, it can often feel lonely doing it. And that's ironic, I suppose. There are professional networks for everyone from tattoo artists to lawyers. There are personal networking opportunities for young moms and avid hikers. But there are few networks to plug into and find other community builders.

If you've felt lonely trying to build a community, you're not alone.

For those who care about building creative communities, a common motivation often emerges from a longing to find "your people" in town. What I've come to discover is that adding your ideas and contributions to your town is an easy way to signal to others what you're seeking. It takes courage to raise your hand and lead, but the reward is finding your community.

Much of the work I've led in State College has stemmed from that place. I've simply been looking for others out there who care about causes I care about. With each new project I launch, I discover a few more of "my people." In doing so, I also fall a little more in love with my town.

I've often wondered if I'm the only one who has felt lonely doing this work. I've wondered if folks in other communities wrestled with how to bring an idea to life and introduce innovation into their town. As I've traveled, I've come to discover that there are lots of people like me in communities all around the world. I've yet to find a suitable directory and you often have to go digging to find them, but they are out there. We are out here, and you just might be one of us!

In 2019, an NPR poll found that 62% of people in rural communities are optimistic that people like themselves can have an impact on their local community. A similar study by the YMCA in the same year found that 87% of young people felt that their small actions add up to creating change, but 74% wish they personally could do more or knew how to get involved. Despite a desire to do so, the challenge is that few know how or where to start when creating change in their community.

As I was paving my alternative path 10 years ago, I found myself having to figure out largely through trial and error what worked. And just as important, what didn't. There were few "How to" guides or 10-step plans that showed me how to build a creative community. After all, community is messy, amorphous, and a difficult thing to grasp. But after successfully running three social ventures and community hubs, I've been able to look back and see what works well when nurturing creative communities from the ground up.

For more than a decade, I've consulted school districts, advised local government leaders, and coached entrepreneurs. I've worked with national foundations and supported emerging leaders at global nonprofits and Silicon Valley startups. But for every individual I worked with, there seemed to be a line of communities behind them seeking help. The demand kept growing.

My hope in writing this book is to provide clarity for more communities than I can physically travel to in a single year.

In it, I'll introduce you to the CANVAS framework I've used to launch all of my ventures. This has served as a guide for countless towns and leaders. The framework was built through practical experimentation over more than a decade of community building work and is informed by many well-known theories, from design thinking to the diffusion of innovation. I've drawn on the wisdom and expertise of those who have been doing this work long before I was even born.

Each chapter in the book focuses on one of six steps in the CANVAS framework. This roadmap will show you how to engage your community, discover pressing needs, rally key supporters, and bring your ideas to life. It will help you follow your curiosity and launch projects that create real change in your region.

My hope is that the framework will help you in the same way that it has helped me over the years.

Along the way, I'll invite you to work on your own community building efforts. I'm a big believer in experiential learning, so if you'd like to simply read through, that's perfectly fine. But if you want to apply the steps as you read, you can get the hand-held Creative Communities Field Guide online (www.mycreative.community) to help you get outside of your comfort zone and apply the framework to your own town. You'll learn about past projects that help illustrate the importance of each step, and I'll highlight community builders in other towns who might otherwise get overlooked.

THE CANVAS FRAMEWORK HAS SIX STEPS

CHART YOUR PATH
Determine what success would look like, how your unique style will influence the idea, and how to move past fears preventing you from getting started.

ASK PROBING QUESTIONS
Get a pulse on what your community needs by getting face-to-face, testing your assumptions, and learning how to ask curious questions.

NAME EARLY ADOPTERS
Identify those who are most eager to rally behind your idea and build momentum by asking for deeper engagement over time and incrementally.

VISUALIZE A PROTOTYPE
Develop moments of wonder, which are small experiments to tangibly test your idea and learn what works. Think small, cheap, and fast to test the boundaries of what's possible.

ARTICULATE YOUR STORY
Design a clear and compelling narrative for your project that stands out and is easily shareable, while leveraging various media forms.

SUSTAIN EFFORTS WITH PARTNERS
Find partnerships that satisfy a mutual need and learn how to lean on your network's trust as a critical currency of partnership-building.

Nowadays, we so often want to get everything we need from a top 10 list or a quick set of tips while skimming the rest. But community building doesn't work that way. The evolution of cities and towns is slow and meandering. Community doesn't always make logical sense and change rarely happens in a perfectly orderly fashion.

After all, your town is not an engine that you have to fix. Your town is a canvas, and you are simply called to add to it. Communities aren't governed by science or math or logic. Communities are an artform that comes to life much like a dancer does on a stage or a painter does on a canvas. All that you must bring is your authentic contribution. And in this book, I hope you find a partner to help you do just that.

Let's dive in!

STEP 1

CHART
YOUR PATH

TEN DAYS INTO OUR CROSS-COUNTRY road trip, as we were driving through Oklahoma, the RV's suspension went out. In the rearview mirror, I saw my passengers bouncing up to the ceiling. I held on to the steering wheel for dear life just trying to keep us moving in a somewhat straight line.

Life has a way of throwing curves that can make it feel like you're out of control. This was one of those. I found myself at the helm of a 40-foot behemoth with minimal experience driving an RV. And despite having a mechanical engineering degree, I knew very little about engines, chassis, or suspensions.

In the swerving vehicle with me were a film crew – editing footage in the back bedroom – and my team. They sat on couches trying to email leaders in the next city, where we were scheduled to visit an alternative elementary school horse farm.

It had been smooth sailing. I enjoyed sitting high above

passenger cars and surveying the road from my captain's chair. Guiding this land-bound ship conferred particular confidence on me. That is until the suspension broke.

At that moment, my focus shifted sharply from the hazy horizon ahead to the painted lines in the middle of the road. Without a working suspension, it felt like the entire vehicle had been thrown onto an unstable trampoline with neighborhood kids jumping annoyingly out of unison. The RV bounced all over the road.

I tried to keep my feet glued to the pedals as the rest of my body bounced violently up and down. Never one to miss an opportunity to innovate, I suddenly envisioned the need for "feet belts." If I were back at New Leaf, I would have hung that idea up on our Idea Wall.

When I finally felt it was safe enough to glance back at my passengers, I saw the look of panic on their faces. Computers were strewn about the vehicle, and the contents of the cupboard spilled all over the floor. A bag of pretzels we'd been looking for emerged from its hiding spot.

Once it became clear we weren't going to die, I felt free to think again about where we were going. Fortunately, we were only 15 minutes away from our next filming location.

I tried to maintain a moderate speed that wasn't so slow as to invite an accident and not so fast that it would send us flying off the road or cause the RV to fall apart entirely. Once I'd dropped the team off at our destination, I Googled the nearest mechanic and took our battered RV to a local garage.

———

Many of us on the team had only met briefly before we hit the road. We were just getting to know each other, one week into a month-long adventure, when the RV's harrowing suspension problems left us stranded in the middle of Oklahoma.

The idea for that road trip had emerged a few months earlier when our group had met. We'd bonded over our shared desire to attend a conference on the other side of the country, along with our lack of means to get there. It turns out that I wasn't the only one sleeping on friends' couches at that time. Most of us were broke, with no way to afford the airfare, let alone a pricey conference ticket.

We commiserated over our shared fate for a few days until one of us had the idea to convince other people to pay us to attend the conference. It seemed like an unreasonable ask at first, but all ideas start that way.

Beyond brainstorming ways to get to the conference, we talked about what else mattered to each of us. We wanted to network and hang out with like-minded collaborators, and learn from others about ways we could improve our communities. And we wanted to embark on an adventure that we could tell our kids about someday.

Most of all, we wanted to have powerful conversations. These are the types of conversations that reveal something that you never knew about yourself, keep you up at night considering new possibilities, and awaken new curiosities. Think of a conversation that's changed your life. Who was it with? What were you talking about? Where were you and how did it start?

People go to conferences because they expect to have those powerful conversations. But often, all you get at conferences are panels, PowerPoints, and free donuts. Powerful conversations rarely happen when you're sitting in an auditorium listening to a speaker.

Rather, it's in the informal, spontaneous, and unplanned moments that you usually find yourself having the most impactful conversations. They happen over breakfast or in the elevator lobby. They happen when you go out for drinks with a new friend or share a taxi on the way to the airport. They happen around bonfires and in backyards. They take place when you don't plan for them, and seldom emerge when you try to force them. They rarely happen in classrooms and offices and conferences. (Although perhaps they happen around those free donuts...)

The irony is that the most powerful conversations in our life happen in the most random of places.

As we realized that, we became less concerned with attending the formal conference. We were more interested in simply meeting people who shared our passion for improving their communities. That's what we craved. That's what mattered to us, and we had a sneaky suspicion we would find those people at the conference.

What's more, we saw no reason the fun should be limited to the few days the conference was being held. Couldn't the journey to the event serve as a great opportunity to have these discussions? That's when the RV entered the brainstorm.

The idea snowballed from there. What if, along the way, rather than eating at fast-food restaurants and getting snacks at gas stations, we met with cool people in their own communities over a meal? What if we brought a film crew along to capture their stories? What if other people paid us to film those stories and share the footage when we got back home?

What if we parked our RV directly outside the conference so we didn't have to go to the formal talks? People could hang out with us between sessions and before and after the conference each day.

From all the "what ifs," Educate 20/20 emerged.

The project's name spoke to our hope of providing a clear vision for what a thriving education system could look like by the year 2020. (Little did we realize back then how badly the world could have used a clear vision for 2020.)

All that brainstorming took place in less than an hour. When you're deeply curious about something, it's hard not to explore questions. Doing so tends to lead to other questions and more discovery until, eventually, you're ready to put an idea into practice.

But first, it's important to get clarity on where you're going, how you'll get there, and understand what's preventing the rubber from hitting the road.

In short, you need to chart a course. To do that, you must:

1. Work backward from the future.

2. Identify your unique style.

3. Reimagine your fears and passions.

✝

CHAPTER 1.1

WORK BACKWARD FROM THE FUTURE

SOMETIMES, YOU ALREADY HAVE DEFINED endpoints and goals in mind when you're charting a path forward. Think of taking a trip where the destination is clear from the beginning. In other cases, you may just want to hit the open road or take a hike and not choose your exact route before setting out. That improvised exploration is what gives the spontaneous journey its meaning.

Regardless of what kind of adventure you plan to go on, as you think of designing a creative community it's helpful to give yourself a benchmark for what success might look like.

———

Before I start any new initiative, I think about what the British philosopher Alan Watts said on the point of living:

"In music ... one doesn't make the end of the composition the point of the composition. If that were so, the best conductors would be those who played fastest; and there would be composers who only wrote finales. People [would] go to concerts only to hear one crashing chord – because that's the end. Same way in dancing – you don't aim at a particular spot in the room; that's where you should arrive. The whole point of the dancing is the dance ... We thought [that] life by analogy was a journey, was a pilgrimage, which had a serious purpose at the end. And the thing was to get to that end. Success, or whatever it is, or maybe heaven after you're dead. But we missed the point the whole way along. It was a musical thing, and you were supposed to sing, or to dance, while the music was being played."

When people talk about community building, it's easy to get hung up on the desired impact and measurable goals. Community builders naturally see something that can be improved upon or enhanced and commit to seeing that change through. But there's more to it than that.

Despite having a similar inclination to enact measurable change, I frequently remind myself that this work is about the art of creating, not necessarily what you create. Community building is relational. It's about people and places rather than numbers and metrics. It's about the dance and inviting others to join you in the performance. It's from that headspace that I like to envision a compelling vision of what my path forward might look like.

Your vision is about where you plan to go. But it's also about what you imagine may take place along the way. When thinking of the journey ahead, what memories do you hope to make? What impact do you expect to have? How will people's lives be different as a result? How will you know when you've achieved your vision? For the Educate 20/20 team, we envisioned having powerful conversations with fellow education innovators leading up to and during the conference.

As you think about your community, you might desire large-scale systemic change. You may not be satisfied until old systems are dismantled and new ones are created. Alternatively, you may envision making subtle changes or having an impact at an individual level. It might simply be that you want to brighten the day of a neighbor you've only crossed paths with a few times.

There's no right or wrong type of vision or scale for your community building goals. As we'll discuss throughout this book, there are many different projects people can take on that will have a meaningful impact on their community.

You'll meet people like Cindy, who installed bird feeders to help older adults build community during Covid-19, and Cornetta, who found creative ways to reframe the story of her city using nothing but bikes and patios. We'll also talk about organizations that have recruited dozens of young creatives to move to and remake their city, and groups that are redesigning neighborhood blocks using lasers and sheets of plywood.

What's important is knowing what community building looks like for you; that way, you have something with which to gauge your efforts as you begin the work.

Your vision may change. In fact, that's expected. You'll take detours and set new destinations in the course of your work. But much like a road trip, your goal at this point is to simply start mapping out where you plan to go and how you'll get there. Then you can focus on enjoying the journey as it begins to unfold.

———————

One of my favorite visions was shared during an interview to hire a director for one of the organizations I support. We needed someone who could organize events, manage logistics, and cultivate a welcoming space for our town's arts community. Beyond evaluating skill sets and resumes, we wanted to get to know the individuals who were applying, so I asked one of the candidates, "When building community, how will you know when you created the impact you hope for?"

Without hesitation, she said she hopes to feel sad when she's done.

Puzzled, I asked her to explain.

She went on to share that if she had to leave this town tomorrow – say, if she got a job somewhere else that required her to relocate – she would be happy to move on. That was because, she said, since moving here, she hadn't been able to find "her people."

But if she got this job, she hoped to create a thriving space where her people – artists, poets, musicians, dancers, and performers – could find their home. This would be a space that was welcoming and inclusive of countless art forms. It would redefine the traditional understanding of art.

She became more animated as she shared her vision. She told me that if we were able to build that together through this organization, when the day ultimately came that she had to relocate, she would feel pretty sad knowing she was leaving something special.

Needless to say, she was hired.

When you consider a vision for yourself, you might use this same litmus test. What would need to happen for you to feel sad about leaving the community you helped change for the better?

———————

When we began charting our path at New Leaf, we knew we would only reach our destination when others were actively participating in community building alongside us. Our mission, vision, and programming frequently changed as we continued to adapt to emerging needs. We evolved from a group focused on sustainability to one that supported social entrepreneurs and then civic engagement. Our central focus was always increasing the number of people actively involved in contributing to our community. We wanted people to carry the New Leaf perspective with them into new parts of our town.

We often reflected on the photos of our town 100 years in the past that lined the walls of the municipal building. The black-and-white images showed old cars along the road and the facades of familiar buildings that still stand today. But there were no people in the photos. They were a static snapshot of bricks and concrete. We had to envision a future that excited us and inspired others to join in our efforts to make our community better.

Clarifying your vision isn't like talking about the weather. Meteorologists are great at forecasting weather patterns. Based on what has happened in the past, they tell us what they anticipate will happen in the future. Past behavior helps predict future outcomes, and that's the basis of forecasting. But when trying to design a creative community, forecasting isn't much help.

Forecasting accounts for the way things have been done before and limits your ability to envision how things might be. This approach constrains your creativity and often results in incremental change. Sometimes you need to ignore those old photos of your town and instead plan based on where you want to be in the future, not where you've been. This is called backcasting. Rather than think about where you are starting from and the patterns that have led to that moment, first determine where you want to be in the future.

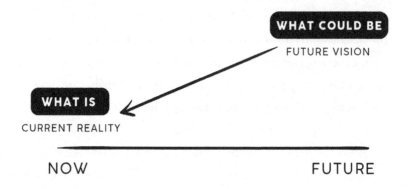

Backcasting from the future.

Create a vision of the future that's so compelling you would excitedly tell a stranger at the bus stop about it. Imagine your community in a way that may feel detached from its current reality, but which energizes you to the point that you feel like skipping down the street as you reflect on what's possible. (At New Leaf, visitors knew I was "backcasting" when I was rolling around the office on rollerblades while playing air guitar with a Swiffer.)

Dream of the possibilities that have yet to present themselves, and imagine a town you would feel sad to leave.

As you get clarity on your vision for the future, backcast to where you are now. What would need to happen for you to reach that future state? What steps are necessary for you to realize that reality?

I have a friend in Houston, Jarren Small, who has a big heart for finding ways to make education more accessible and engaging. Now, there are a lot of constraints that make it difficult to redesign the education system. But Jarren has a way of ignoring the way things have been done in the past and dreaming into the future.

One thing he noticed was that kids in his community were often disengaged at school. However, when the topic of music came up, kids jumped right in. Many shared their admiration for rappers they looked up to as cultural icons. So Jarren began pondering what a future would look like if rappers ran the education system. What if learning felt more like a concert? What if rappers taught their English class?

Compelling visions are often wrapped up in enticing "what if" questions.

Jarren began to map out ways he could answer his "what if" questions. He shared his vision widely with others. Soon enough, "Reading With a Rapper" was born. The initiative brings rappers into the classroom and uses socially conscious lyrics to teach kids about concepts ranging from metaphors to hyperbole.

Jarren transforms the classroom by bringing in a DJ mixer and lighting up the walls to feel like a concert, and he partners with technology companies to give each kid headphones and tablets to follow along with the lyrics. His team has built a curriculum that schools can use, and at the end of a few weeks, they bring in well-known rappers to teach the class.

Designing creative communities requires leadership. There is perhaps no greater skill for a leader to possess than the ability to inspire forward-thinking visions of the future.

Leadership experts James Kouzes and Barry Posner have dedicated much of their careers to studying what constitutes a good leader. In the Harvard Business Review, they shared one of the critical discoveries they made:

"In an ongoing project surveying tens of thousands of working people around the world, we asked, 'What do you look for and admire in a leader (defined as someone whose direction you would willingly follow)?' Then we asked, 'What do you look for and admire in a colleague (defined as someone you'd like to have on your team)?' The number one requirement of a leader – honesty – was also the top-ranking attribute of a good colleague. But the second-highest requirement of a leader, that he or she be forward-looking, applied only to the leader role. Just 27% of respondents selected it as something they want in a colleague, whereas 72% wanted it in a leader. (Among respondents holding more-senior roles in organizations, the percentage was even greater, at 88%.) No other quality showed such a dramatic difference between leader and colleague."

Beyond honesty – a trait that is important for leaders and followers alike – the ability to create a compelling vision that you can backcast from is the single most important trait that will position you as a leader.

As you consider what your vision looks like for your community, give yourself permission to ignore the constraints of your current reality, and dream about a future that hasn't been created yet. Once you can see that future in your mind, you'll be able to chart a path to lead the rest of your community there.

With Educate 20/20, we had a vision for our project. Now we had to figure out how to get there.

IDENTIFY YOUR UNIQUE STYLE

THE SECOND COMPONENT OF CHARTING your path is identifying your unique style.

We all create change in our own way. Some of us are charismatic visionaries. Others prefer the pragmatic supporter role. You might see yourself as a behind-the-scenes kind of leader, or you may instead be comfortable being out front. I thrive disrupting systems from the outside, whereas my wife's strength lies in changing systems from within.

Taking stock of your strengths and how they can best be put to use to advance your vision will help you when thinking about who you want to partner with and how to design something that's ultimately fulfilling. An idea may sound great, but it has to be something you're motivated to put your energy into, or eventually, you'll get frustrated and quit pursuing it.

I love how Elizabeth Gilbert describes ideas in her book "Big Magic: Creative Living Beyond Fear":

> *"I believe that our planet is inhabited not only by animals and plants and bacteria and viruses, but also by ideas. Ideas are a disembodied, energetic life-form. They are completely separate from us, but capable of interacting with us – albeit strangely. Ideas have no material body, but they do have consciousness, and they most certainly have will. Ideas are driven by a single impulse: to be made manifest. And the only way an idea can be made manifest in our world is through collaboration with a human partner. It is only through a human's efforts that an idea can be escorted out of the ether and into the realm of the actual."*

Ultimately, ideas are asking us to step alongside them and our style needs to align with theirs. You might discover an amazing idea, but it's not the right fit for you. That's OK. There's nothing to be ashamed about; it just means that idea is waiting for another person with different strengths and styles to bring it to life.

What you shouldn't do is succumb to pressure (internal or external) to run with an idea that doesn't suit you. I once made that mistake with a friend. He bet me I couldn't make money running a Bubbleball soccer company. For those who aren't familiar with Bubbleball soccer, this involves wearing a giant inflatable bubble suit, attempting to play a game of soccer, and crashing into your friends at full speed.

Having a hard time saying no to things, I shook on it, found a supplier in China, and ordered the equipment 24 hours later. It took me four years to make my investment back, which I considered a win. The idea was never entirely aligned with my style. Yes, I'm the kind of guy that people might expect to own a Bubbleball soccer company. It excited me enough to hit 'buy' on the spot. But had I thought more about my own preferences and strengths, I may have had a bit more hesitancy getting into it.

For starters, I don't do risk management very well. Health and safety issues aren't my strong suit. That's why I have lawyer and insurance friends nowadays. So owning a company that regularly puts people at risk of sustaining a concussion probably wasn't a great idea right out of the gate.

I never enjoyed making people watch safety videos, and I frequently questioned whether I should allow the older gentleman to get in a ball and square off against younger rugby players. Soon enough, I came to resent having to clean and deflate all of the equipment after a game and that most of my clients were overnight youth group lock-ins, as someone who very much values getting my sleep. You can only deal with so much sweaty teenage energy at 3 a.m.

Suffice it to say, I ultimately gave up on the venture, and moved on to other ideas that better fit my style and interests.

Identifying your unique style is like picking your preferred mode of transportation for a trip. Driving an RV across the country is much different from an interstate bike ride or flying from coast to coast.

In the same way that we selected an RV as the way we would explore the country, when we began charting our path for Educate 20/20 we asked ourselves what our unique style and strengths were on the organizing team. One theme that emerged was that we were all storytellers. We loved the idea of discovering hidden stories around the country and spending time asking curious questions to learn from others.

We also learned that many of us were connectors. We liked connecting people, places, and projects. By taking a road trip, we could put this skillset into practice and help others we met to do the same.

Finally, we knew that we all cared deeply about education. We were interested in the history of alternative learning spaces, disruptive and transformative teachers, and organizations working to reimagine the higher education system as we knew it.

So we took into account those three components – our passion for education, storytelling, and facilitating connections – to form our group's unique style. Rather than picking a project first and letting that dictate our approach, as is often done, we let our strengths and style as a group determine the nature of the project.

———————

There are plenty of personality tests and frameworks that are used to provide clarity on your style, from Myers-Briggs to StrengthsFinder. I'm generally personality test agnostic, but have found that there are often two simple questions that, when answered, can help you unlock your style. What do you care about? What are your skills?

When you combine your cares and skills, you are more likely to pursue work you're uniquely qualified for that truly matters to you. This is how you identify your unique style.

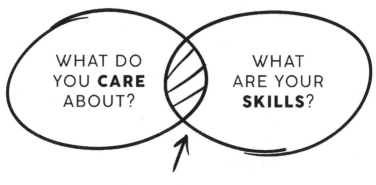

YOUR UNIQUE STYLE

Identify your unique style by combining your cares and skills.

During our Educate 20/20 trip, we discovered a group early on that inspired how I think about our cares and skills. One of our first stops was in New York City. Lugging our camera gear in hiking backpacks and suitcases through Grand Central Station, we dodged tourists and business people on the subway as we tried to squeeze multiple interviews in with organizations spread out across the city.

One of those organizations was Echoing Green, which identifies, supports, and invests in emerging social entrepreneurs around the world. Social entrepreneurs are folks leading organizations that reimagine systems and create transformative change. Some of the most driven and inspiring vision-casters I know are connected to the Echoing Green community.

One of the frameworks they use to help people discover purposeful work is called Head + Heart = Hustle. Head represents your skills. Heart represents your cares. And your Hustle indicates your unique style.

Each year, I take a sabbatical and journal about my cares and skills to make sure that I'm continuing to do work that aligns with my unique style. You can get creative in combining your cares and skills to see how they best align. These are some of the questions I often reflect and journal on, inspired by Echoing Green's framework:

What do you care about?
- What makes your heart beat faster, from love, anger, or joy?
- What causes and culture – like movies, books, TV, and TikTok – do you engage with the most?
- Have you ever stood up for anyone in the past? What motivated you? What happened?
- What social or environmental problem do you ache to see solved?

What are your skills?
- What do you do well?
- What education (traditional or nontraditional) do you have?
- What have you learned from your work? Both things you would put on a resume and things you wouldn't are pertinent.
- What three things do you do best?

Once you have both lists, simply pick one thing from each list and imagine what it would be like to combine them. They don't have to make sense – it's merely a time to brainstorm fun possibilities for what you might pursue. If you find you're not sure where to begin in determining how you can make an impact in your community, reflecting on these questions may unlock new paths for you to explore.

Many years ago, I was guiding a group of emerging leaders through the framework, unaware of the transformative potential it might have on their lives. One of the participants, Brandi, was quietly working on a large sheet of poster board we had laid across the floor, mapping out her various lists. She'd circled potential ideas, scribbled notes across her sheet, and starred the word "Morocco."

Later that evening, our retreat was coming to a close, and it was time to hold our final ceremonial party. But this wasn't any ordinary party. It was a reunion party for our future selves. Before the party started, we guided the group through a meditated visualization to imagine what their life might look like 10 years in the future if they had fully pursued the life they dreamed of. We then invited everyone to attend the party as if they were their 10-year-older self.

The party was lively. Participants mingled excitedly, talking about where they were living, what they were working on, and what it took for them to get to this point in life – all made up, mind you. It was playful and interactive, much like the New Leaf cardboard party.

As I bounced around the room, I found myself talking to 10-year-older Brandi. There was a sparkle in her eye. Before I could get my question out, she exclaimed that she was living in Morocco. She excitedly described her home and the neighbors she regularly hung out with. There was a renewed confidence in her voice as she shared how she had pursued her vision of supporting artisans and building community in Morocco. Granted, this was all an elaborate improvisation of a party and Brandi's future self persona was one that she'd dreamt up, but the moment still felt real for her.

A few months after the retreat, Brandi moved to Morocco. She had previously planned to obtain certain degrees and jobs to amass the credentials and experience to pursue her dream. But she found a shortcut, and instead moved directly to Morocco. She planned to learn through firsthand experience what it would take to build a social venture and create community. Fast forward 10 years, and Brandi has been an active contributor to her Moroccan neighborhood, starting food trucks, travel blogs, and fair-trade e-commerce sites, all with the hopes of strengthening her community.

By focusing on her cares and skills, she could chart her path forward to find her unique style. By taking the time to sketch out where you are going and how you'll get there, you are more likely to be engaged on the long road ahead. A Gallup Poll found that when managers took their team's strengths into full consideration, the ratio of engaged to disengaged team members was 60:1. But when managers ignored their team's strengths, that ratio reversed to 1:12, with far more disengaged team members.

In mapping out your unique style and pursuing work that matters in your community, it's essential that you focus on what excites you so that you have the energy to engage with the work fully. Gallup has found that "people who use their strengths every day are three times more likely to report having an excellent quality of life, six times more likely to be engaged at work, 8% more productive and 15% less likely to quit their jobs."

Getting clarity on your cares and skills will give you the necessary energy to truly enjoy the road ahead. It'll also make it less likely you quit when things get difficult. As your journey begins, you will be required to take a leap of faith. Being keenly aware of your style will help you muster the courage needed to step into the unknown and be a leader in creating change in your community. As Nelson Mandela reflects:

> *"I learned that courage was not the absence of fear, but the triumph over it. The brave man is not he who does not feel afraid, but he who conquers that fear."*

So what does it take to reimagine and conquer those fears?

CHAPTER 1.3

REIMAGINE YOUR FEARS AND PASSIONS

AS WE DEVELOPED A CLEARER understanding of our vision and style, the plan for Educate 20/20 came into focus. We would get an RV and travel the country, spotlighting leaders reimagining education, from preschool to medical school. We would bring a film crew along to capture our interviews and travel to the education conference on the West Coast. There we could interview attendees and hang out, so we didn't have to pay for a conference ticket.

We fundraised and plastered stickers of donors' faces on the outside of our RV. (We only found out later how surprisingly difficult it was to remove these stickers when the trip was over; the silhouettes of supportive neighbors and loyal parents are now permanently imprinted on the side of that vehicle.) We reached out to leaders in cities across the country to develop a roadmap and timeline for where we would stop along the way. Soon enough, we found ourselves loaded up in the RV on our way to New York City for the first stop of many.

There was only one problem: None of us had ever traveled coast-to-coast in an RV before.

We were abruptly reminded of this when during the first five minutes of the trip – before we even made it on the highway – we drove the RV into a field of wet grass and got stuck. We had hoped to take a celebratory photo commemorating the start of our trip. Instead, we were promptly fined by the police for destroying private property, and had to get towed by a friend with a large truck. That set us back five hours, and didn't help our confidence.

When we finally made it onto solid ground, I glanced back in the side mirror. There were deep grooves in the dirt and the flashing lights from the police car reflected off the nearby buildings as the officer finished writing the ticket.

As hard as we tried to shake it, we all had this annoying fear in the back of our minds that we weren't going to be able to pull this off. Who gets their RV stuck and gets fined five minutes into a month-long road trip? Honestly, there must be someone else more qualified to lead this.

We've all felt that before: imposter syndrome. Research published in the International Journal of Behavioral Sciences estimates 70% of Americans experience imposter syndrome at some point in their lives.

As you begin charting a path and exploring ways to enhance your community, you're likely to wrestle with these kinds of fears. Rather

DESIGNING CREATIVE COMMUNITIES

than trying to ignore, fight, or succumb to these fears, I've found it's most helpful to acknowledge and even be thankful for them.

When you experience imposter syndrome, it signals you've stumbled upon an idea that means something to you and will stretch you. If you didn't care about the idea and it wasn't something that pushed you outside your comfort zone, you wouldn't experience imposter syndrome. So whenever I feel that fear begin to sneak into my psyche, I pause, acknowledge it, and thank it for reminding me that this is an idea worth pursuing. Having this mindset has helped me grow as a leader and better understand what I'm capable of creating.

The Echoing Green team describes this in terms of the "fear means go" mantra. When you come across fears that point to your insecurities or self-doubt, those fears can be treated as gifts because they tell you what to do next: to go! Move in the direction of the fear because that is an area where you can grow further.

Although I use the common descriptor imposter syndrome here, I no longer think of this kind of fear that way. Instead, I refer to it as my "What's Worth Doing Signal."

As I drove our RV around the country for an entire month, it seemed like every time I looked in my side mirrors, I could see the police lights from that first night. The flashback was a constant reminder for me that this was a project worth doing. Over time, when we deal with what others commonly refer to as imposter syndrome this way, we find that we're able to put our fears in their proper place until they fade away like mile markers in our rearview mirror.

A few weeks before leaving for our Educate 20/20 road trip, I read these words from Elizabeth Gilbert. Little did I realize at the time how relevant they would be for the following month.

59

"Dearest Fear: Creativity and I are about to go on a road trip together. I understand you'll be joining us, because you always do. I acknowledge that you believe you have an important job to do in my life, and that you take your job seriously. Apparently your job is to induce complete panic whenever I'm about to do anything interesting – and, may I say, you are superb at your job. So by all means, keep doing your job, if you feel you must. But I will also be doing my job on this road trip, which is to work hard and stay focused. And Creativity will be doing its job, which is to remain stimulating and inspiring. There's plenty of room in this vehicle for all of us, so make yourself at home, but understand this: Creativity and I are the only ones who will be making any decisions along the way. I recognize that you are part of this family so I will never exclude you from our activities, but still – your suggestions will never be followed. You're allowed to have a seat and you're allowed to have a voice, but you are not allowed to have a vote. You're not allowed to touch the road maps, you're not allowed to suggest detours. You're not allowed to fiddle with the temperature. Dude, you're not even allowed to touch the radio. But above all else, my dear old familiar friend, you are absolutely forbidden to drive."

But what if you don't even know where to start? Most of the time, our fear can make identifying where to begin feel overwhelming. If you're one of the lucky ones, you may have already stumbled across an idea you want to pursue. But for many of us, the prospect of finding an idea worth pursuing in the first place is daunting.

Whenever I start to experience this fear of the unknown, I'm reminded of a dirt path I walked in Tanzania many years ago around the base of Kilimanjaro.

It was my first time traveling independently, and I had arrived in Arusha, Tanzania without much of a plan. I wanted to learn from other cultures how they nurture and value community. I flew there with a high school friend, but we went our separate ways once we touched down. Upon arriving at the airport, she was immediately greeted by smiling representatives from the organization she was working with – all wearing matching polo shirts and holding a sign with her name clearly written on it. She had signed up to work with a well-established organization, so her path was clear.

I, on the other hand, had no concrete plans. Two more friends were going to meet me in a few days, but I had no idea where I was going to sleep or what I would be doing until then. I'd made contact before my trip with someone you might loosely describe as a guide, but I had no idea what to expect. No one was holding a sign with my name on it.

The reality of what I had gotten myself into set in soon, as my friend left with the group of volunteers she'd joined. She glanced back over her shoulder at me one last time as I sat on the floor of the airport with no clue what my next month would look like. I waited for what felt like hours debating whether I should leave the airport on my own, or suppress the urge to panic, and wait for my transportation to arrive.

After what felt like an eternity, a van pulled up. The driver rolled the window down and called out, "Are you Spud?" Thrilled to hear my name, I jumped up with my backpack and approached the van. A man stepped out as he slid the door open.

"Hi, I'm Paradise," he told me. "Follow me!"

With that, the adventure began. For the next week, I followed Paradise around, thinking this had to be a sign from the heavens. I mean, his name was Paradise. Who was I to argue?

On the second day, he took me high into the forest surrounding the base of Kilimanjaro. As we drove around the tallest mountain in Africa, we passed countless small trails and winding paths that I imagined all somehow led to the peak. I thought about my hometown, the paths others had cleared for me without me knowing it; and the words of mythologist and author Joseph Campbell: "You enter the forest at the darkest point, where there is no path. Where there is a way or path, it is someone else's path; each human being is a unique phenomenon. The idea is to find your own pathway to bliss."

I didn't know it then, but with each new experience, I was slowly finding my own path to designing creative communities. I look back now and see the path through the forest. But in my early days as a community builder, it felt like I was entering the forest at its darkest point, and only discovering the path as I walked.

We unloaded in a small village, and Paradise introduced me to a local Maasai warrior. He told me that for the rest of the day, I should follow him. He didn't speak English. I didn't speak Swahili. But that didn't seem to concern Paradise as he jumped back in the van, waved, and drove off.

For the next 10 hours, I hiked in silence behind my new friend. We passed cornfields and small villages, walked along creeks and deep into forests. I had no idea where I was going, but with each new turn of the trail, I was overcome by the beauty of the country and the mountainside. At the same time, I recognized that I was clearly following a well-worn path that he had walked many times before.

With no way to communicate, I spent most of the time watching the Maasai warrior's feet ahead of me, mesmerized with where he would lead me. It started to feel effortless as I gave little thought to where we were heading. But as the sun began to set, I realized that I might never see Paradise again. I was utterly lost, alone and at the mercy of a guy with a big spear.

Fear started to creep into my mind as it got dark, and we approached a cow auction in the middle of a large field. But just when I was starting to map out possible escape routes and determine what it would take to lasso a cow and ride it to safety, Paradise emerged from the crowd. "How was your day?" he smiled.

Sometimes I wish that discovering ideas was as easy as following Paradise. I've lost count of how many people have advised me to simply follow my passion, which always comes off as wishful thinking. You've likely been given similar advice. It's as if you only need to find what you're singularly passionate about and the rest will be effortless, like following a guide on a well-worn path.

I get why people say it. It sounds inspirational and uplifting. It's meant to encourage you to pursue the things that truly matter to you. And it seems like noble advice when you're trying to chart your path.

The problem is that very few of us know precisely what we're passionate about. It's likely that not even the person who told you to follow your passion knows theirs. If following your passion was as easy as following Paradise, we would all be able to simply enjoy the journey and not worry about where we're going.

I've met a handful of people in my life who are genuinely passionate about one thing. My guess is you can think of one or two people in your life who are that way. But that's rare, and such people are hard to find. For most of us, although we like to pretend we know what we're passionate about, we're still searching and hoping to stumble across that one true thing.

The very notion that we need to identify some singular passion to live our best life puts a ton of pressure on us. That's often why people fail to get started in the first place when trying to contribute to their own community. They're paralyzed by this kind of weighty expectation and worried about failing or looking foolish if it all comes crashing down.

Fortunately, there's a simple fix. You can shrug off all that pressure and still pursue meaning and happiness in your life by slightly adjusting the approach. Rather than trying to follow your passion, follow your curiosity instead.

You may not know what your passion is, but I've yet to meet someone who isn't curious about something. The critical starting point for anyone who wants to create change in their community is genuine curiosity. By first considering what you're genuinely curious about, you can chart a path forward.

Not only is following your curiosity an easier starting point, but it also leads to more opportunities for innovation. In a 2018 study conducted by Stanford psychologists Carol Dweck and Gregory Walton, alongside Paul O'Keefe from Yale-NUS College, researchers found that students who were passionate about one specific issue were less likely to develop new ideas because they could not connect ideas across interest areas. "Many advances in science and business happen when people bring different fields together, when people see novel connections between fields that maybe hadn't been seen before," Walton notes.

The researchers described those who followed their passion as having a fixed mindset, whereas those who followed their curiosity and developed a passion were seen to have a growth mindset. Having a growth mindset allows an individual to innovate and overcome challenges more easily. Those with fixed mindsets who were solely passionate about one area had more difficulty navigating new areas of interest when the material was complex and challenges arose. However, those who embraced their curiosity were able to more easily navigate different and difficult fields.

As I reflected on my time with Paradise, I wasn't following him because I was singularly passionate about what he was doing. I only knew the guy because I stumbled upon his email on a shady website. I followed him because I was genuinely curious to see where he would take me, what he would expose me to, and how he would expand my worldview. I ventured off to Tanzania with the hopes of learning about community from the ground up, and Paradise stepped in as the guide to that curiosity.

When we started Educate 20/20, I was genuinely curious about what the future of education would look like. I also wanted to know what it would be like to take a cross-country road trip. And I was curious to see if I could actually drive an RV without breaking down. (As it turns out, that's not my top strength.)

If I were passionate about those things, I still would be living in an RV and devoted solely to education work. But I'm not. Curiosities come and go. They enter our lives at just the right time, often packaged as questions.

But when we inquire, and let our curiosity take us where it may, it opens new doors. Ultimately, though the point is to follow your curiosity, pursuing those new ideas just might lead you to discover something you are passionate about as well.

———————

After we had the RV's suspension repaired, my team hit the road again en route to California. By this point, friends were learning about our grand adventure and calling to see if they could hitch a ride to the next state.

It wasn't long before we had a dozen people crammed in the RV. At night, everyone scrambled to find an open spot to sleep. (I'm sure we were also breaking a seat belt law.) I found myself engaged in powerful conversations with each new passenger as I drove on and people rotated into the coveted shotgun spot.

We had our fair share of comical moments.

Our poop pipe – yep, that's a thing on an RV – exploded in New York. This happened as one friend attempted to unload the RV at a rest stop. The blowout covered him from head to toe as the rest of us watched in horror. Having dealt with my fair share of poop pipes at New Leaf, I tried to advise him on cleanup while sitting safely inside the RV with the window up, trying to contain my laughter.

We got stuck making a hairpin turn on a cliff in California, and were left to perform an impressive 100-point turn. We drove to NASA in Texas and hung out with astronauts, our RV dwarfed in size by the massive rocket sitting outside the parking lot. We joined in on fiddle concerts in Oklahoma, went "cosmo tripping" with the head of the Buckminster Fuller Institute in North Carolina, and learned about the importance of vision quests in New Mexico.

We knocked out a power line while driving through North Carolina, which blocked the road in front of us. With darkness setting in and very much not wanting to be stuck there for the rest of the night, we hoisted our friend on the roof with a big stick so that he could lift the cable over his head. He did this as we drove underneath, and he walked slowly with the stick and cable above his head. Not our wisest decision. It was another one of those moments where my lawyer would have frowned.

Fortunately, we found out later it wasn't a live power line, and simply a television cable line. But the story sounds a lot more exciting when you envision it as a live power line, buzzing with electricity and danger.

The trip was a whirlwind of connections and excitement. In 35 days, we traveled more than 7,800 miles, visited 16 cities, and interviewed 45 community builders and education innovators. As we looked back on our vision and what was originally important to us, we realized we'd accomplished our primary goal: to have lots of powerful conversations. We also got to go to the conference for free.

We met some of our side goals too, though others fell by the wayside.

Despite having hundreds of hours of footage, we never ended up producing a film as we had hoped. We just never got around to editing what we'd filmed. It turned out that none of us were super passionate about starting a production company.

But new business partnerships and collaborations emerged that we hadn't anticipated. And that's where we put our energy instead.

That's how ideas roll. They take on a life of their own and evolve as you pursue them.

As you're thinking about the contribution you want to make to your community, the first step is always to sit back and chart your path. You need a roadmap.

But that doesn't mean you can't ever change course, as we literally did traveling across the country. Your community will influence and shape your work, and the plan will naturally evolve. Your role is simply to be curious, follow your idea, and make adjustments as your vision and the needs of your community change. And to do that, you need to learn how to ask really great questions.

STEP 2

ASK PROBING QUESTIONS

ASKING QUESTIONS CAN OPEN DOORS. It can also lead to doors being shut in your face. But with persistence, the right questions can lead to valuable connections and insights to help you make meaningful change in your community.

Early on in my community building career, I was in Washington, D.C., visiting my friend Adam. Whenever I travel to major cities, I'm reminded of the stark differences compared to the smaller towns where I typically work.

State College is a town of 100,000 people, half of whom are college students. As a community builder, I've met many local business owners and nonprofit leaders, and I frequently recognize people I see just walking down the street. It would actually be a challenge to get groceries without seeing someone I know.

But taking in a larger city from the backseat of a taxi, I can't help but be awestruck by the sheer scale of it all. So many businesses, nonprofits, and organizations are needed to make metropolitan centers what they are. I can only imagine everyone who is busy at work in high-rises I pass, and wonder at the diversity of roles people need to take on to keep society moving forward.

My first social venture was in New York City, and after it spectacularly fell apart (a story for another book), I moved back to State College. With a fresh perspective, I quickly came to appreciate how much easier it is to wrap your arms around a small town than a large city. I'm not alone. There is a growing wave of interest among young creatives to contribute to a rural creative renaissance.

The Ewing Marion Kauffman Foundation, a well-known funder and catalyst of entrepreneurship efforts around the country, reported in 2020 that millennials were increasingly moving to smaller communities and rural towns. They highlighted a Pew Research Center study which found "that more urban (30%) and suburban (35%) residents are interested in moving to a rural community than rural residents (20%) are interested in moving to an urban community, an increasingly possible trend in light of [2020]."

By sheer size, small towns often aren't so complex that you don't know where or how to start when creating change. When I think about a city versus a small town in creative terms, it's the difference between painting a mural versus sketching in a journal. When I draw in a journal, I just put pencil to paper. I'm not intimidated by the scale of what I'm doing or at a loss for where to begin. I'd say the same applies to doing community building work in a small town. But a city is this vast canvas. Even in its simplest abstraction, it's like a giant, empty wall. Where do you start? How do you make a measurable impact? It's not always so clear.

Although I marvel at big cities, I find that I enjoy small

towns. They have this incredible potential that invites residents to contribute to the community's identity. But frustratingly, big cities on the coasts are often held up as exemplars whenever talk turns to innovation. Those reference points and models don't always translate well to changemaking in smaller communities.

As I caught up with my friend over lunch in D.C., we talked about how small towns are ripe for innovation and explored the overlap between my work and his. Lunch went by quickly, and I walked Adam to the elevator lobby of his fancy office building to say goodbye. Just as I was getting ready to leave, I saw other organizations' names in the high-rise listed next to the elevator and noticed one I recognized.

Ashoka, an organization dedicated to advancing social change, was also located in the building. I'd always been inspired by their collaborative approach to innovation. But in my daily experience, they were nothing more than a great website with an excellent newsletter, and a group I often referenced at New Leaf.

When Adam asked what had caught my attention, I told him about my admiration for this organization and how cool it was that he worked in the same building as they did. "I would love it," I said, "if there was a group like this in State College that I could randomly drop in on and chat with on my lunch breaks."

That's what you do in small towns, you drop in unannounced.

"Why not do that now?" Adam suggested.

He had a point. But this was D.C. People carry briefcases and wear fancy suits. All I had on were some dark jeans, an untucked white button-down shirt and my iPad.

"That shouldn't matter," Adam encouraged, as he nudged me in the elevator and pressed the button to the 20th floor, where

Ashoka's office was located. He stepped out, smiled, and off I went.

Alone in an elevator, on the way to meet with an organization at the top of my "Cool Groups to Meet Someday" list, that familiar friend, imposter syndrome, kept me company.

I got off, approached the floor-to-ceiling glass-walled office, and mustered as much confidence as I could. If this would work in State College, who's to say it wouldn't work in D.C.?

I knocked on the door and the receptionist unlocked it as I stepped inside.

"Hi, I'm Spud. I was wondering if I could talk to someone at Ashoka about what you do in education?" Friendly, open-ended, and to the point. That's what I was here to do. It seemed like a straightforward enough question to ask.

The receptionist gave me a slightly disapproving smile, and I soon found myself being escorted back out into the hallway. I don't recall us having anything that resembled a real conversation, and I was starting to worry that I severely overstepped by boldly walking into their office unannounced. Standing outside the elevator doors once more, the staff person walked back into the glass fortress as it locked behind them.

Thoroughly confused, I waited. Maybe someone will join me out here. But as my confidence began to wane, I took advantage of the little bit of fleeting courage I had left and went back to the glass door and knocked. The lady behind the counter glanced over and begrudgingly opened the door once more for me.

"I'm sorry, but I'm a little confused. Should I wait out there for someone?" After all, I'm a small town guy, so I didn't know how this big city stuff worked. "No," she replied. "As we've said before, we don't take solicitations from tech salesmen."

I was puzzled. Then I glanced down and realized, with my iPad under my arm and dressed in an untucked button-down shirt, that I looked like the stereotypical tech guy.

"Oh no! I'm sorry, I'm not here to sell anything. I'm genuinely curious and just interested in talking to someone and learning more about what you do." With that, our shared misunderstanding evolved into her genuine confusion.

"No one has ever just wandered in off the street asking to talk to us," she replied. I was right: This is not how things are done in cities. I knew I needed a briefcase. But her confusion quickly dissipated, and she asked me to take a seat in the lobby. She dialed someone on the phone as I prepared to get escorted out once more.

Instead, to my delight, she called up one of the founders of their university division – the same program I happened to follow most closely online. I was taken directly to the co-founder's office, and we met for over 90 minutes. We talked about the work we were doing at New Leaf and how that overlapped with work Ashoka was pioneering. She invited me to attend their upcoming conference and introduced me to a few folks she thought I should know.

As fate would have it, one year later, I would find myself trying to attend that same conference for free. And those people she connected me with – they were the ones who traveled with me on the Educate 20/20 RV to get there.

––––––––

Asking great probing questions is the step that takes you out of your head and into the streets. This step is all about getting uncomfortable and talking with as many people as possible to discover their needs and desires, unlock their connections and visions, and begin getting the pulse of your community.

To do this requires persistence and a healthy dose of courage. Sometimes your questions will lead to progress, and at other times you'll feel like you're getting nowhere. But if you wait until you have it all figured out, you'll never move forward.

You will fail every time if you focus solely on your idea and not on the people your project will ultimately benefit. And the only way to improve your understanding of who your idea will help is to talk with members of your community about it. After all, your goal is to have a positive impact in your town, not simply launch an idea. Those two things can often get conflated. This step helps you focus entirely on others to strengthen your idea and test the kinds of assumptions we all naturally carry into the process.

To complete this step, you'll need to do the following:

1. Get face-to-face.

2. Test your assumptions.

3. Spark creativity with curiosity.

CHAPTER 2.1

GET FACE-TO-FACE

A FEW YEARS AGO, WHILE driving, I noticed trash bags piled high along the road that were bursting with color. Curious about what was spilling out, I pulled over.

To my delight, the bags contained thousands of those colorful balls you find in children's ball pits. Ecstatic about my discovery, I crammed as many of the balls as I could fit into my car, moving my unimpressed dog to the front seat to make room for our find. We drove away as the colorful balls spilled over my headrest.

Days later, the $10 inflatable pool I'd purchased online arrived at my doorstep, and I was ready to hit the streets.

Armed with my pool, thousands of balls, and my pockets filled with sharpies, I went down to our main street. I inflated the kiddie pool and wrote #BallpitofIdeas in big, black letters on the outside. Then I jumped in the pool.

If I were passing someone on the street casually lounging in a ball pit, I would naturally stop and ask what they were doing. Most, however, didn't seem so curious. Many who passed me chose to put most of their energy into avoiding eye contact. They pretended like there was nothing to see here. But I could be steadfast as well. So as streams of people walked past me, seemingly uninterested in what I was doing, I just kicked back and waited.

Soon enough, someone stopped and mustered the courage to ask what was going on. I invited that person to join me in the ball pit and write down an idea they had to improve our community on one of the balls. It could be anything: a rock climbing gym, colorful sidewalks, or free pizza every Friday. My goal, I told that first person who was curious enough to ask, was to cover every ball with an idea.

My first participant pondered and awkwardly attempted to get in the kiddie pool without sending balls rolling down the street. (In all honesty, I kind of secretly hoped an incident report would be filed describing the whole scene.)

Besides collecting ideas, I was also curious to talk with people who joined me in the ball pit about their experience in town. What do you do for fun? What kind of events do you enjoy attending in State College? When have you felt most connected while living here?

I soon found myself engaged in meaningful conversation with other community members, and a crowd of people gathered around, sharing their ideas on colorful balls.

Unfortunately, in the 21st century, many of us hide behind our technology. We can easily make it look like we're doing work or are otherwise preoccupied, even when we're not. But if you want to give an idea legs, you have to do more than the bureaucratic minimum, which is to simply send out a survey. You must spend time building relationships. You need to get face-to-face to get the pulse on your community. For me, that meant sitting in a ball pit.

Don't get me wrong: If my focus here was inspiring top-down leadership, we could talk about surveys, committees, and hierarchies (and there are far too many things that are more fun to write about than that). But my interest lies in inspiring community building from the ground up.

As Margaret Wheatley and Deborah Frieze share in their book "Walk Out Walk On: A Learning Journey into Communities Daring to Live the Future Now":

> "Despite the fact that community is inherently local, most people engaged in community change nonetheless aspire to follow in the footsteps of big business by scaling up, expanding programs, and rolling out offices in new geographies.

To meaningfully impact your community, you have to get out from behind a screen and engage with others face-to-face. Imagine trying to learn how to dance by reading an instruction manual; it wouldn't work. Dance requires being experiential and engaged. It's the same with community building.

In a 2017 study published in the Journal of Experimental Social Psychology, researchers asked 45 participants to each approach 10 strangers and ask them to fill out a survey. Each participant used the same script, but half of the group made their ask face-to-face, while the other half relied on email.

Before the participants began reaching out to strangers, the researchers asked them to predict how many people they expected would comply and fill out their survey. Participants in the face-to-face group estimated five of 10 would, and participants in the email group estimated five or six. Both groups expected roughly the same rate of return, but the outcomes were drastically different.

The researchers found that requests made face-to-face were 34 times more effective than emailed ones. In other words, for every six people you engage with face-to-face, you would need to email more than 200 people to get the same response.

One of the researchers, Vanessa Bohns of Cornell University, noted in the Harvard Business Review that "people tend to overestimate the power of their persuasiveness via text-based communication, and underestimate the power of their persuasiveness via face-to-face communication." Whether we are requesting someone to share their feedback, donate to a cause, or sign a petition, we wrongly assume that we will get the same response rate regardless if we engage face-to-face or through digital tools.

A ball pit may not be your style, and that's entirely understandable. As hard as I've tried, I still have yet to convince my wife, Katie, to jump into the ball pit on the street with me, although she has written her fair share of ideas on the balls. I like creating moments of surprise and intrigue – that's my style. But you may take a different approach. Whatever you do, just don't rely solely on email or an impersonal survey to gather feedback.

Instead, set a goal to talk with three people this week on the phone. Start with people you know. Grab a notebook and jot down insights from each conversation. Then aim to talk with six people next week, with half of them being people you've never met before, and so forth. You can schedule video calls. You can meet people in the streets. You can hang out at a coffee shop and talk to passersby.

Or you can invite them into your ball pit.

The method is up to you, but your goal is to spark a conversation. The most valuable insight always emerges from open dialogue, never from digital data.

———————

You can connect with people in your community and learn about what others want in ways that fit your unique personality and style.

One day, Katie and I were reflecting on all of the extra space we had with just the two of us living together. A large part of what attracted us to one another was our shared desire to host and bring people together. After we bought a house, we were in a better position to do just that. So we mapped out how we each wanted to use this new asset.

Katie loves to host people with food. From waffle bars to sushi roll parties, food is central to the way she entertains. She loves a good cheese board at a potluck.

I, on the other hand, have an insatiable appetite for hearing about other people's ideas. So when I host, I sometimes wear a fanny pack stuffed with sticky notes and sharpies, because you can never be too prepared for a good brainstorm.

As we reflected on our very different hosting approaches, it struck us that there was no reason we couldn't find a creative way to combine them. What if we hosted a potluck brainstorm? People could bring food to share, and we would have workshops to get people thinking creatively about ways to better our community while they ate.

As someone who has lots of ideas, it's easy to get distracted. So if I discover an idea that I think is worth pursuing, I buy the domain. I call it my Idea Tax, and it costs me about $8 per idea per year.

I once bought www.changemakingis.sexy and had planned to sell calendars of social entrepreneurs lounging on the couches they slept on while launching their ventures. It was meant to be tongue-in-cheek, with all the proceeds supporting various nonprofits. Despite thinking it was a great idea, I never did anything with the domain and after paying the Idea Tax for nearly a decade, I realized it was time to move on to other projects.

After my wife and I came up with our new hybrid hosting plan, we bought www.PotluckBrainstorm.com, with no idea what it meant, and slept on it. A few days later, the idea wouldn't go away. It clearly wanted to be given a chance.

So we built a website, invited anyone in our community over to our house, bought 1,000 branded magnets with a logo we'd quickly designed, and waited to see who would show up. The first time we had a dozen people come over. These were our early adopters. (We'll talk more about early adopters in the next chapter.) We spent the evening having great small group discussions, and by the end of the night, we'd filled our stomachs with food and covered our tables with ideas.

There was a lot of excitement to continue the conversations. So we picked a day when we could do it all over again the next month. Word spread, and more people joined us. Cars lined our sleepy street as we got into the routine of hosting monthly Potluck Brainstorms. All we were missing was a Yelp page with business hours for our home.

The purpose of each event was simply to listen to the community. What needs did people have? What excited other community members at the moment? Where did they see opportunities for improvement? Which of their current frustrations could we transform into new possibilities?

Each month we would pick a different topic, from local food to reimagining faith communities, supporting the arts or bridging political divides. We would find someone well respected in each of those topics in town and ask them to invite all of their friends and colleagues. We wanted to get a representative pulse of our community, and to do that required reaching outside of our immediate friend group. When probing your community, you must find ways to connect with people who aren't in your circles.

According to a 2018 poll conducted by the Pew Research Center, more than two-thirds of Americans only know some or none of their neighbors. Of those that do know their neighbors well, 58% do not meet for gatherings or get-togethers.

Meaghan McDonough of the Boston Globe highlights how these findings reveal a disturbing trend. "In 1974, 30 percent of Americans spent time with their neighbors more than once a week, and just over 20 percent never spent time with their neighbors. Two generations later, things have flipped; almost 35 percent of us never spend time with neighbors, while less than 20 percent do so more than once a week."

Not surprisingly, rates of loneliness doubled from 20% in the 1980s to 40% in 2017. We trust each other less as a result; where half of Americans reported trusting others in 1970, less than one-third did in 2020. "Strikingly, the U.S. is the only established democracy to see a major decline in social trust," Kevin Vallier, a professor of philosophy at Bowling Green State University, wrote in a 2020 essay on our distrustfulness in the Wall Street Journal.

As we connect less with our neighbors, our society also reckons with the role that racial injustice, gender inequality, and unconscious bias play in our communities. As a straight, white male, I recognize the privileges I've been afforded in society. It's all too easy to surround myself with others who think and look like me. When attempting to lead in a community, it's critical that you acknowledge your bias and actively seek out diverse perspectives. Without that intentionality from Day One, you won't get an accurate pulse of your community, and at worse your efforts to improve where you live could actually be destructive.

Our monthly Potluck Brainstorms were a way to connect with our community, and we intentionally sought out diverse perspectives. The evening always kicked off with a potluck and encouragement for visitors to eat with someone they didn't know. It didn't matter if you brought a fancy international dish or a bag of chips. Everyone was welcome. We had tables and chairs scattered in small clusters around the house, with no more than five people in a group so that everyone's voice could be heard.

As people finished eating, we would transition to three rounds of brainstorming. I provided an overview of the topic and shared our intention to discover how people in the community were feeling regarding that issue. As everyone briefly introduced themselves, I reminded them that we hoped they would form at least one new connection by the end of the evening with someone else who shared a desire to create positive change.

For each of the three rounds, participants were given a specific question to discuss in their small groups. At the end of a round, one person would stay in place as a host, and everyone else rotated to a new group and picked up on the themes from the previous discussion.

By the end of the evening, we would all come together and share what insights, ideas, and connections we'd made. Inspired by a process called World Café, this technique can be used with lots of different types of groups. Over the year, we began to hone in on what kind of questions best solicited creative, new thoughts and connections.

The brainstorming usually went something like this:

Round 1: We'd pose a question that was designed to get participants to focus on the current reality of their town, such as:

- **Arts**: What do you most value about our local arts scene?
- **Faith**: When you consider reimagining faith communities, what conversations do you ache for that you wish you had more often?
- **Homelessness**: What are some inspiring ways homelessness is being addressed globally? How are we addressing this locally?

Round 2: We'd ask a question that inspired the group to envision their community in the future or from an alternative perspective, such as:

- **Arts**: Imagine our local arts scene 10 years from now, when everything is just as you wished it could be. What is different, and how have you contributed?
- **Faith**: How would an alter ego, like Rosa Parks, design your ideal faith community?
- **Homelessness**: Pick two random nouns from a hat and use them to inspire creative solutions for how we might reimagine our approach to solving housing insecurity in town.

Round 3: We'd pose a question that motivated the group to move toward taking action to improve the community, such as:

- **Arts**: What prototype could you launch in the next few months that would bring us closer to that "dream local arts scene"?
- **Faith**: How might we creatively integrate those "alter ego" approaches into our existing faith communities in Centre County?
- **Homelessness**: What could we do in the next month to begin to implement one of your creative solutions?

By the end of the year, more than 400 people had come to our cozy home to have a meal and engage in these brainstorming sessions. Many entered as strangers but left as friends. Business partnerships and new relationships were sparked as folks met one another.

We didn't set out to start a formal thing, but by the end of the year, folks around town knew about the Potluck Brainstorm and were encouraging their friends to sign up. (Though, I never managed to get rid of all of those magnets; I still find them in drawers and bags strewn around my house.)

When considering how to ask probing questions of your community, you need to think about an approach that aligns with your style. Katie and I did this by hosting Potluck Brainstorms. These started small, but grew into large, intentional listening exercises. Regardless of how you approach this step, the primary objective should be to spend quality time talking with your community.

Albert Einstein once famously said, "If I had an hour to solve a problem, I'd spend 55 minutes thinking about the problem and 5 minutes thinking about solutions." If you're a math genius trying to describe gravity, that's a great approach when staring at your blackboard by yourself. But if you're working on launching a project to improve your community, I would suggest tweaking that approach: If you have an hour to solve a problem, spend 55 minutes talking with your community and 5 minutes coming up with a solution together.

With the Potluck Brainstorm, we spent 11 months talking with our community and listening to their needs, and one month reflecting on what we heard to begin creating our solution together.

One of the main themes we identified was the need for a physical space for local artists and creatives. Our gathering in July focused on the local art scene was one of the most well-attended and engaging discussions of the year. Many attendees reflected on how they longed to have these conversations on a more regular basis and wished that there was a creative space – apart from showing up unannounced at our house – where that could happen.

Ultimately, this process of regularly gathering and connecting led us to ask one more question to test an assumption: Would people engage and step up if we were to pursue the next step of launching a dedicated space for arts and innovation in town? The answer was a resounding yes.

As you get face-to-face with your community, pay attention to patterns and themes that emerge in conversations, and use these opportunities to test your assumptions.

CHAPTER 2.2

TEST YOUR ASSUMPTIONS

KIDS ARE SOME OF MY favorite teachers. They help me unlearn the unhelpful things adults teach each other. This was most clearly on display when a group of high school students wanted to put a slide in their library.

I was helping a rural school district in Pennsylvania transform two of its libraries into innovation centers. Think of "Extreme Makeover: Home Edition," but for a library. We even had a film crew. It was a bold undertaking. My team had less than a week to design, renovate, and haul out tens of thousands of books to transform the libraries into engaging spaces for students to learn, form ideas, and collaborate.

Before wielding our sledgehammers and paintbrushes, we spent two days meeting with teachers and students to get a sense of how they wanted to redesign their space.

I had a team of professional designers, innovation consultants, and construction experts with me. No one would have argued if we'd just laid out a blueprint with our design and paint swatches. That's how they do it on TV after all.

They would have trusted us to lead the process, but there would have been no long-term investment and engagement. We would have rallied some early supporters, but the project would never have felt like their own space over time. That's the beauty of co-creating, or collaboratively designing and implementing an idea with others.

So we started the week with a series of workshops designed to probe the teachers and the students and make them the experts. We told them that they would be designing their spaces; we were just there to listen and follow their lead.

Often people have a hard time putting words to their experience, perspective, or vision. In the same way that it can be challenging to formulate creative questions, it can be tough sometimes to verbalize thoughts. This is where images are helpful.

We printed out enlarged Pinterest boards featuring photos of brightly colored innovation spaces and nontraditional learning centers. Everyone received stickers to vote on the pictures that most excited them, based on how they wanted their library to look and function at the end of the process. We pulled the images that received the most votes off the wall and taped them to a large piece of cardboard. Then we sat down to talk with the group about why they selected the spaces they did.

Some of the innovative spaces selected resonated with teachers and students alike. They both wanted a mix of open space and private nooks. They both wanted a space that felt organic, natural, and relaxing. But there was one polarizing picture.

Every time we guided students through the process, they selected the picture of a slide. A slide is the last thing that most people expect to see in a library. The teachers never selected this image. They were too focused on optimizing space and having plenty of storage. When we told them the students all picked the slide as one of their top images, the teachers came up with similar reasons for why we assumed they chose it.

What kid doesn't like a slide? Of course, they're going to pick it, even if it's not practical. It was tempting to don our expert badges and justify why we could toss out the slide picture. But had we done that, we would have missed out on a critical insight.

We paused and dug a bit deeper. "What is it about the slide that excites you?" we asked the students. We wanted to better understand why they had selected this, rather than assuming we knew the reason.

Lots of the kids giddily smiled at one another. They all knew the slide was easily the coolest photo on the board. Finally, a girl who was one of the quieter students raised her hand from the back.

"If we want the library to become a place for new ideas and creativity, then I want to be reminded that crazy ideas are encouraged. A slide doesn't belong in a library – which is why I like it. I want this to be a place where I can share my ideas that might not belong anywhere else in school, the ones that may sound silly or look out of place."

Then another younger student chimed in. "And if this is a place where we are supposed to think creatively, it would be nice to have something to climb high up on so we can look down and make sense of the chaos with our ideas."

So much for the adults wearing the expert badge. It was time to hand that over to the kids.

We assumed that they picked the slide simply because all kids love slides. But there was so much more meaning and depth to their selection than we would have imagined.

Still, I tried to justify why the slide was impractical. I explained to the students that I loved their reasoning, but a slide would be difficult to pull off with a limited budget. We didn't want to settle for a cheap plastic slide, and we definitely couldn't afford to custom-fabricate a metal slide. So as brilliant as their reasons were for having a slide, we didn't have the money to pull it off. That's what adults do; we think of the reasons why a good idea can't work.

Feeling content with myself – that I had found a way to hear the students out but reasonably explain why we couldn't pursue such an impractical idea – I got ready to close the workshop. Then another student raised her hand.

"So ... my dad likes to make custom-fabricated slides as gifts for neighbors. I texted him, and he said he would be happy to make us one, and build it this weekend for us for free. Would that be OK?"

Just like that, the students went from expert designers to expert construction managers. They had managed to not only come up with a brilliant design idea and support it with sound reasoning, but they had managed to find free materials and labor to build it.

The best way to test your assumptions going into a project is to make your community the expert. And when you do so, be prepared to be surprised.

You will talk with people who may have assumed they didn't have input in the process, and find that they have great insight and resources to contribute. People crave opportunities to engage and be heard. When you enter the conversation by making them the expert, you shift the power dynamic to signal their participation is not only wanted, but central to the community's success.

Unfortunately, the slide didn't get built because it rained throughout the renovation weekend. But we worked with the students to find other ways that they could build climbable furniture and be reminded that their ideas belonged in this space.

After a few sleepless nights, we finished the renovations. (TV shows make it look far too easy.) On the day of the grand reveal students proudly climbed on top of bookshelves that were built for that purpose and surveyed the scene. They could see their ideas reflected in the space before them.

To test your assumptions, you must remove yourself and your ideas from the center of a project. Make others your focus to avoid simply validating your own idea.

Had I learned to do this earlier in my career, I might not have spent so many hot days on the sidewalk with a cardboard tube shoved in a Christmas tree stand.

I was working on a creative placemaking fellowship, honing an idea I proposed called "Innovation Trailheads." Think of the signs you see in vacation towns with colorful wooden arrows pointing to random cities and listing the mileage to reach those destinations. Mine would be similar, but instead of showing random cities, they would point community members to innovation spaces around our town.

Most people wander our streets without realizing how many

unique groups exist in our downtown, such as makerspaces, co-working offices, arts and craft studios, and entrepreneurship incubators. Over the last few years, local entrepreneurs created some amazing spaces, but they remained hidden, and many people didn't know they existed at all.

I envisioned these "Innovation Trailheads" would serve as a wayfinding tool to help people discover meaningful ways to get plugged-in to our creative economy. On each trailhead, I would put a touchscreen that allowed people to view videos and photos of each space, hopefully lowering the barrier of walking into a space that felt unknown to them.

I had $5,000 to start producing the guideposts. But I knew from experience that I needed to first talk to community members to make sure I was spending that money wisely.

So I found a large cardboard tube, and taped arrows to it. I wrote some details about the cool organizations around town on the arrows, and shoved it in a Christmas tree stand. I had my prototype (which we'll talk more about later), and took it out to the sidewalks.

I stood around the corner and eagerly watched as folks walked by. Who needs $5,000? I could just get my raw materials from a dumpster and put my cardboard-construction skills to good use.

To my surprise, not a single person batted an eye at this strange contraption that stood in the middle of their path. Time and again, people effortlessly dodged the cardboard tower without looking up from their smartphones. It was quite impressive.

For a few weeks, I stubbornly attempted to validate my idea rather than listen to my community's actual needs. Slowly I discovered that although funders and big organizations like our

Downtown Improvement District thought these trailheads were engaging, people on the street paid no attention to them. Thankfully, I still hadn't yet spent $5,000 on a bunch of touchscreens, concrete, and wood.

It took me a bit. I'm stubborn and don't back down from my ideas sometimes – which I'm working to change. But soon, I was able to distance myself from the Innovation Trailhead idea.

As I talked with folks, I pivoted subtly. I removed my idea from the center of the conversation. Initially, I had been asking, "What do you think of the idea of having physical trailheads on our sidewalks that point people to innovative spaces around town?" Then I reframed the question to focus on others: "What is the biggest challenge for you when it comes to getting meaningfully connected to our community?"

Few people will tell you to your face that your idea is bad. (Except for that one friend we all have who is brutally honest and lacks any finesse or compassion.) When we frame questions that indirectly ask people to tell us if they like our idea or not, we are setting ourselves up for dishonest feedback. We're not actually collecting the insight needed to build solutions that address root issues.

Often utilized in the field of design thinking, reframing is a powerful community building tool when testing assumptions. If I were to ask people to draw a vase, most of the drawings would look quite similar. We all have an idea of what a vase typically looks like. But if I reframed the prompt and asked everyone to "draw a way for people to enjoy flowers in the home," the images I would receive would look wildly different. Through a simple reframe, we generate far more constructive, innovative, and valuable insight.

As I reframed my ask, it didn't take long before a pattern

emerged. I started asking, "Where do you go to find community, and how did you discover that group?" Those I spoke with told me over and over again that a single person had pointed them toward their core community. It could be a friend or neighbor, a boss or colleague, a mom in their kids' playgroup, or a real estate agent they met when shopping for a new house. Almost anytime someone discovered "their people," it seemed that it was a result of another person going out of their way to personally guide them toward that community. The person was the guidepost.

Unspoken in all of this was the implicit discovery that those who didn't feel that sense of belonging hadn't met that person who could help guide them to their group. A sign, flyer, or arrow isn't what helps someone discover community. It's a trusted person – a guide – who does this.

Once I came to this realization, I changed my entire approach. Instead of installing physical trailheads, I began to develop an organization called Trailhead. This group would be a community of trusted guides in town who could help people discover how to find others locally who shared similar interests.

To problem-solve in your community, you need to get close to the problem. You must learn as much as you can about the issue and be ready to part with your original idea.

A 2019 poll by CBInsights analyzed 101 startup failures to determine the most common reasons why a project didn't get off the ground. Ideas failed for many reasons, from poor marketing or the wrong team, to lack of funding or getting beat out by a competitor. Among the 20 reasons that the team at CBInsights analyzed, the top reason for a startup failing – accounting for 42% of the failures – was that they didn't test their assumptions.

In other words, these ventures' leaders assumed the market – the community they hoped to serve – wanted what they were creating. The report noted, "tackling problems that are interesting to solve rather than those that serve a market need was cited as the No. 1 reason for failure."

According to a similar study conducted in 2020 by Wilbur Labs, a startup incubator in San Francisco, founders said the most important advice to prevent failure was to do more research before launch. This just reinforces the need for spending time testing assumptions about the problem you hope to solve.

One of my favorite community builders and justice pioneers, Bryan Stevenson of the Equal Justice Initiative, puts it this way:

"You cannot be an effective problem-solver from a distance. There are details and nuances to problems that you will miss unless you are close enough to observe those details."

I have a good friend, Tessa Zimmerman, who runs a social venture that helps students manage anxiety during high school. Her organization creates tools and frameworks that help students better care for their mental health. Tessa often shares that to identify the root needs her organization addresses, she has spent countless hours hanging out in high schools. She jokes that she could have received a second diploma because of all the time she has spent in high schools.

Apprenticeships represent one of the oldest forms of learning, and at the same time, are becoming the new hip thing in education. We're learning that rote memorization and preparing for standardized tests are not the best ways to learn. Frequently kids and adults retain more when they learn by doing alongside elders and peers.

It's the same with community building. We're taught that developing strategic plans and studying academic theory is the best way to redesign communities so that they thrive. But it turns out, the best teacher of all is the problem itself that you want to solve.

If you want to create change, forget the textbooks and committees. Get out in the streets and learn firsthand what you're up against. Apprentice with the problem. Talk with people who experience that problem. Changemaking is an action-oriented and experiential process.

One of my colleagues who helped spearhead the library renovation project with me was also working with a state agency trying to redesign its policies on homelessness. They were creating conferences and panel discussions to hear from experts. They had stacks of white papers and theory to dig through. But when my colleague asked them if they had spent time talking with anyone homeless, the room went quiet. She suggested that those experiencing homelessness should be invited to the events, and the organizers got visibly uncomfortable. They had never even entertained the possibility of involving the people who experience the problem firsthand.

We've become so accustomed to studying community issues from a sterile perspective that we don't realize the inherent flaws in this arm's length approach. It's easier to try to solve homelessness when it's an abstract concept, rather than a community you interact with in a personal way.

Apprenticing with the problem is uncomfortable. Testing your assumptions requires getting face-to-face with people experiencing the exact problem you are working on. That demands time, effort, and sometimes placing yourself in difficult and unfamiliar situations.

As you learn from your community, ask yourself where you can physically hang out that will surround you with the problem you ultimately hope to solve. Ground-up solutions require being on the ground. Sitting at your computer Googling potential fixes isn't enough. You need to go into your community to improve it. Then your next step is to have the courage to ask curious questions.

CHAPTER 2.3

SPARK CREATIVITY
WITH CURIOSITY

HOW MANY TIMES WHEN MEETING new people have you been asked a familiar question like "What do you do for work?" Despite the depth of our personalities and experiences, many of the questions we ask one another do nothing more than scratch the surface.

Few of us are taught how to ask really good questions. Or, more to the point, it seems we've forgotten how to be curious.

Curiosity is one of the most critical ingredients for fostering human connection. George Mason University psychologist Todd Kashdan has spent much of his career exploring the role that curiosity plays in building relationships, and in the Greater Good Magazine he shares:

"Being interested is more important in cultivating a relationship and maintaining a relationship than being interesting; that's what gets the dialogue going. It's the secret juice of relationships.

"When you show curiosity and you ask questions, and find out something interesting about another person, people disclose more, share more, and they return the favor, asking questions of you. It sets up a spiral of give and take, which fosters intimacy."

A good friend and colleague of mine, Chad Littlefield, is an expert at asking really curious questions. I asked Chad to officiate my wedding when Katie and I got married in Mexico. He wasn't your traditional officiant, and leading up to the wedding, he recounted to us details of his wedding day. Everything was flying by; the months of planning and all the nervous excitement had led to a blur of an afternoon. Many married couples experience a wedding day just like it.

After the ceremony, he was greeting guests in the receiving line when a friend of his walked up to him, put his hands on his shoulders, and simply asked, "Are you present? Because you don't want to miss your own wedding."

At that moment, the day came into sharp focus for my friend. A simple question, stated with purpose and intention, helped him to take everything in that day.

As community builders, the questions we pose to our neighbors have a similar ability to help people see the blur of the town around them with a new and sharper perspective.

Because we couldn't bring everyone with us to Mexico, Katie

and I hosted a wedding reception in our backyard for local colleagues and friends later in the year. Along with celebrating our love, we wanted it to be an opportunity for people to have great conversations and build new connections. Since most of us struggle with asking strangers curious questions, we staged a game that would help guests overcome this common anxiety.

As everyone arrived, we had a deck of cards at the entrance, and each card had a question on it designed to spark connection. We grouped guests based on how they knew us, such as the bride's college friends, work colleagues, and the groom's family. Each time someone asked a question to a guest who was part of a different team, they received a point for their team. Every hour we awarded prizes to the team that had asked the most questions to guests from other groups. Or, at least, that's what we'd planned to do.

As it turns out, our guests weren't as interested in our well-crafted friendship-building game as we were. The lure of winning cheap sunglasses just wasn't enough. They were far more interested in sampling the different cupcake flavors Katie had made.

But the game wasn't a complete flop. Halfway through the party, I walked inside to the kitchen to fill our cooler with ice. Before I turned the corner, I heard a group of kids chatting. None of them knew each other, and they were standing in a tight circle surrounding two kids in the center. The room got quiet. They didn't realize I was standing around the corner, as I'd paused to eavesdrop. With intense curiosity, a 9-year-old in the center of the circle broke the silence as he asked a 6-year-old standing next to him: "If you had 10 years left to live, how would you live life differently?"

Silence. And then, as if channeling his much older self, the

6-year-old responded: "I would probably start working out more and eating better."

As soon as the answer was out of his mouth, the entire circle cheered. "Yay, we got another point!" And the kids ran off to get more cards with questions they could ask one another. From that point on, we awarded the sunglasses and prizes to the kids at the top of each hour.

Kids have so much to teach us about how to build community. Their curiosity, laughter, and willingness to dive headlong into whatever they do are exactly what is needed when designing creative communities. As author Bob Goff writes in his book "Everybody Always: Becoming Love in a World Full of Setbacks and Difficult People":

> *"[Kids] aren't afraid of the things many of us are afraid of. Their curiosity about what they don't know outdistances their fears about what they do know by a mile."*

Asking probing questions allows us to fully embrace our inner child. Sometimes all we need is a deck of question cards and permission to go out of our way to ask curious questions to strangers.

One helpful tip for asking curious questions is to always start with how and what questions, which will often lead to why. You may have heard of the technique of asking "five whys" to get to the core of why someone acts and thinks the way they do. But often, you need to crack the door open with a how or what question first. In going deeper, you'll discover why as the conversation progresses.

When talking with community members, I often try to ask a question from each of the following four categories.

Get to Know Them: questions that help you better understand the specific individuals you aim to help, such as:

- What's the most challenging part of your week?
- What do you wish you had that doesn't exist yet?

Identify the Real Problem: questions that ensure you are solving the root issue, not just symptoms, such as:

- Tell me about the last time you had an experience with [the problem you seek to solve]?
- What are you already trying as a solution?

Test Potential Solutions: questions that invite feedback on the initial ideas you might have, such as:

- What would stop you from using this solution? Budget? Time? Not interesting enough? Better alternatives?
- On a scale of 0-10, how likely are you to tell your friend about this solution? Why?

Check Your Gut: questions that help you review what you heard and allow you to stay connected, such as:

- It sounds like X is hard/important to you, but Y is not. How accurate is that?
- Do you know anyone else who might have this problem that I could ask similar questions to?

Your goal is to learn as much as you can, rather than validate your pre-existing ideas. Feel free to ask for feedback on your proposed solutions, but keep an open mind and be sure to welcome critique. Much like a ball pit on the street, frame your curious questions in a way that simply invites others to dive in and contribute their own ideas.

In doing so, following your curiosity will not only test your assumptions, it will also lead you to develop more creative solutions. One of the most fascinating studies on this was done by NASA and a team of researchers led by George Land. They were interested in measuring the creative potential of NASA employees and wanted to know where creativity comes from and how to nurture it.

Researchers tested 1,600 kids between the ages of 4 and 5 and found that 98% of them scored at the genius level – a measure of their ability to develop novel solutions to problems. They were shocked to discover that nearly every kid is born a creative genius.

But the study went on to test the same group of kids five years later. At that point just 30% of the kids registered at a genius level. And when they tested them five years later, in their early teens, only 12% were found to be creative geniuses.

Fascinated with the declining results, the researchers administered the test to adults and found that only 2% tested at genius level.

What is happening that causes us to grow out of creativity as we age? The researchers made an important discovery. They found two types of thinking:

- Divergent thinking, which is when we come up with new and imaginative ideas.
- Convergent thinking, where we assess and judge the practicality and usefulness of novel ideas.

Both types of thinking are necessary. The problem, however, is that our education system teaches us how to do both kinds of thinking simultaneously. We are expected to brainstorm and evaluate the potential of new ideas all at once. In doing so, we hamper our imagination – and that results in a decline of our creative potential.

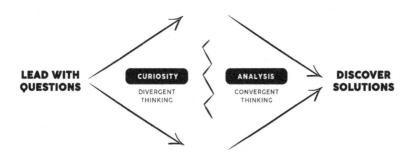

Curiosity is the difference between divergent and convergent thinking.

Crafting curious questions helps you momentarily step away from convergent thinking and lets your brain freely entertain new possibilities.

For adults, it's only natural to want to start diving into the logistics or reasons why a suggestion is or isn't possible in your community. As you engage in dialogue, encourage yourself to temporarily hit the pause button on your desire to analyze ideas from your community. Learn, don't validate. Listen with an open mind, free from judgment.

I love how Peter Himmelman, author of "Let Me Out: Unlock Your Creative Mind and Bring Your Ideas to Life," describes it:

"When we fully immerse ourselves in joyous doing – as opposed to anxious mulling – we can become more creative."

Asking interesting questions has been shown to help teams discover original ideas, reduce group conflict, and minimize how likely we are to fall prey to confirmation bias or stereotyping.

Approaching your community with the curiosity and playful spirit of a child will help you not only test your assumptions, you'll also meet people who are excited to get more involved in your work.

Asking questions face-to-face allows you to build relationships and develop social networks. A survey won't do that. Once you make those connections, the next step to turn your idea into a solution is to identify early adopters.

STEP 3

NAME EARLY ADOPTERS

I'VE ALWAYS WANTED TO BE in a secret society. I can see why some people might have concerns about being blindfolded, led into fields or dark basements, and taking secret oaths. Nonetheless, I've long had a desire to be a part of something underground.

Sadly, I've never been invited into a secret society. And that's why, a few years ago, I set out to create my own. It turns out, you need to be good at keeping secrets to enter a secret society, or start one. And it's no secret that I'm not very good at keeping them. But I've never let a minor challenge stand in the way of my dreams.

My partner in crime – whose identity I shall never reveal – and I designed a secret emblem. (OK, it was Christian Baum, a childhood friend and my business partner on many ventures.) We built a "hidden" website, or at least used URLs no one would ever search, and left clues around town. We mapped out the plan on the back of an envelope and met in secret locations away from our normal gathering spots.

We had a new university president starting at Penn State, so we did our best to pin the secret society on him. If people were going to start asking questions, he was going to take the fall for us. I still don't think he knows that he was the inspiration for such a spectacular underground organization.

In seeking out an inconspicuous domain that no one would ever find, we decided on the latitude and longitude coordinates of our town's center: www.407914n778586w.com. Then we bought the same mysterious domain names for all of the cities our new university president had previously lived in or been employed. If people were going to go digging, which we fully expected and hoped would happen, we needed to create a digital papertrail to keep them off our scent.

The secret society was called the Rebel Alliance. (I can only imagine that we had recently watched Star Wars.) The goal was to help community members find – though secretly – other creative community builders and changemakers around town. Each member of the secret society received a sticker with our emblem and was instructed to place it on the bottom corner of their office door. If you were part of the secret society and saw a door bearing the emblem, you knew that inside was someone you could trust as a co-conspirator.

When you begin your journey as a community builder, no one hands you a little black book of key contacts. But we were about to change that – discreetly.

We came up with a list of our top 20 rebellious friends in town and mailed them each a silver envelope with a melted wax seal.

The letter was our form of induction because we couldn't risk revealing our identity too soon. We mailed ourselves letters as well and joined the fun of being surprised just like everyone else. Each letter invited the inductee to nominate one or two people into our ranks through our obscure website. Selfishly, this would be a pretty clever way to grow our personal network because we were the ones that saw all of the responses.

Well, it turns out that lots of people are bad at keeping secrets. Maybe there's a reason secret societies use blindfolds instead of letters to drive the point home. Word of our mysterious group quickly spread.

To our frustration, no one followed the clues we'd left implicating the university president in bringing this organization to town. I suppose university presidents have more important things to do. But if I ran a college, I would put creating a secret society at nearly the top of my to-do list.

Our vision for establishing a thriving network of underground changemakers never materialized. Very few, if any, of our inductees nominated new friends, which meant those friends we expected would get an invite were never asked into the inner circle. Then they got upset that they weren't invited. Things spiraled from there, and I had to pretend I was in the dark about all of it.

I don't know who spilled the beans, but our secret society was quickly losing its all-important shroud of mystery and sense of community. As it turns out, we have a pretty distinctive graphic style when it comes to designing logos, so everyone immediately knew we created the emblem. People just played along for a few weeks before spoiling our fun. Despite months of behind-the-scenes planning, our secret society became a public failure.

———————

We learned the hard way that rallying your community and finding early adopters for your idea is the opposite of building a secret society. Naming key people who want to help make your vision a reality should always be public and inclusive, never private and exclusive.

We got distracted with the idea of amassing an extensive network of influential friends and forgot the group's original intention.

As a community builder, you must always focus on what's best for your town. If you're in this work to push your own agenda or simply grow your black book of contacts, you're setting yourself up to be disappointed.

I've come to learn there are far more effective ways to find early adopters than building a secret society. The nice thing is that there is some predictability in how you can grow your network without having to mail a bunch of secret envelopes to hopeful prospects.

Unlike powerful conversations that seem to happen spontaneously, ideas spread somewhat predictably. Yep, you read that right. There's actually a bit of science that helps us understand how ideas spread.

If you've ever seen Derek Sivers'TED Talk called "How to Start a Movement," you know what I'm talking about. If you haven't watched it, you may want to pause here for a moment to do that. It's short and quite entertaining.

Sivers describes a video taken at an outdoor music festival as he plays it for the TED audience. It features a "lone nut," as Sivers describes him, dancing by himself. And by dancing, I mean he's busting a move like you would if you had little rhythm and no concern for what others think. The guy flails his arms as he follows his own drumbeat.

A crowd of his peers looks on, until suddenly someone gets up and joins the lone nut. This is the first follower, and he tries to mimic the leader's dance moves. There's some rolling on the ground, and a bit more arm flailing follows as the music plays on. The crowd takes in the spectacle, appearing unmoved at first. Then a few more people join, and a few more, and suddenly a massive impromptu dance party breaks out on the lawn. The lone nut became a movement – but only because of the first follower.

That's how ideas spread. As Sivers points out, leaders often get all the credit, but you must have followers to start a movement. The same is true for turning ideas into projects, and projects into initiatives, which evolve into organizations. You need followers, not just a leader. (In fact, as Sivers notes, without followers, a leader is just a lone nut.)

Thankfully, followers are somewhat predictable. In our own lives, we play a mix of roles; sometimes we follow, and other times we lead. When it comes to cooking, I'm definitely a follower. As soon as I veer away from a recipe, I've entered the danger zone – it turns out you can't mix spices simply based on if their colors match well. My wife, on the other hand, excels at creating her own concoctions in the kitchen. There's never been a recipe Katie has encountered where she can't find a way to go off-script and still make it taste good.

When it comes to fog machines, however, I shine as a leader. I have more fog machines in my basement than most people have lamps, and I'm often consulted on how to best optimize a space or event with fog. If you've got a murder mystery party coming up,

I'm your guy to give it a little pizzaz!

If you're reading this book, you likely want to tackle a community building project or aspire to take the lead in improving your city or town in some way. Congratulations, you're the lone nut (cue waving your arms frantically above your head). Now to become a leader, you'll need to find your first follower.

The first follower is the person that lends credibility to an idea. As you begin testing assumptions for what is truly needed in the community, a first follower comes alongside and essentially says, "I believe in this idea and am willing to stand behind it" (or dance alongside you, say, if you're at an outdoor music festival).

To attract others to join a budding movement, a first follower doesn't need lots of influence or power or charisma. They just need a network of friends, which most people have.

Once you have your first follower, you can recruit others from their network, and then attract more followers from those networks, and so on. Eventually, you reach a tipping point where momentum builds, and your idea has transformed into a movement. That's the goal of this step – to intentionally build momentum.

To achieve this, you'll need to do three things:

1. Find your first followers.

2. Stagger incremental asks.

3. Build momentum through trust.

FIND YOUR
FIRST FOLLOWERS

THE THEORY SUPPORTING THE FIRST follower video, which is far more entertaining than academic literature on the concept, is called diffusion of innovation. Oddly enough, Katie and I bonded over this very concept on our first date. We're that kind of couple that likes to geek out together about behavior change theory. So naturally, I have a special place in my heart for this concept.

In any case, diffusion of innovation is a social science theory used to explain how an idea diffuses, or spreads, from one person to the next and ultimately throughout a population. This framework maps out how different segments of a community might respond to new concepts, and to what extent they are likely to follow an idea.

Most people fail at getting an idea off the ground because they too often start looking for partners (which comes later in the

CANVAS framework) instead of people who want to be followers. There is a difference. Naming early adopters is not the same as finding partners. Partners are often organizations, and they come with stipulations and formalities, whereas followers are simply engaged individuals.

Think of this stage as trying to find a few good friends to join behind you. Just as if you were leading a conga line at a dance party, your goal is to find the people willing to grab onto your shoulders. Focus on building relationships, not developing partnerships.

If you were trying to build something in a bureaucracy, it would make sense to start with partners. That's the traditional top-down approach. Someone has an idea, a committee assembles, that committee forms a subcommittee, and each develops a research paper on who knows what. Then your idea dies. Bureaucracies are good at killing ideas.

To breathe life into an idea, a bottom-up approach is almost always more effective. If you focus on finding partners, you're likely to miss attracting followers who are critical in building the base of your support. Most partners have an old guard, bureaucratic mindset. That's useful later to sustain an idea, but not now. At this stage, one loyal follower is worth more than 10 pledged partners.

The diffusion of innovation is a simple bell curve broken roughly into three categories: early adopters, the majority, and laggards. The curve represents how likely someone is to adopt an innovation over time. At the front of the curve lies first followers.

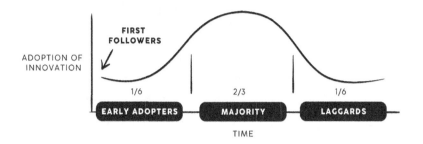

The diffusion of innovation curve illustrates how ideas spread.

A laggard is one of the last people to adopt a new idea, product, belief, or innovation. In communities and local government, laggards are sometimes referred to as CAVE people. Citizens Against Virtually Everything. You likely know the type: people who don't like change or disapprove of new ideas. CAVE people are often quite outspoken and loud in a community. They show up to all the town halls, making it seem like there are more of them than you think. But laggards only represent one-sixth of the population. That's the good news for anyone searching for that first follower and early adopters.

Most of your community falls somewhere in the middle when it comes to adopting innovations – they're not early adopters or laggards. The majority like to embrace new ideas once they've seen them validated by others. These people are great because once you reach them, your idea has really begun to spread. But early on, they aren't your target group.

At this stage, your goal is to figure out how you can reach early adopters. This is where you will find your first followers. These are the people who will naturally find ways to leverage their influence and position – regardless of how prominent, small, or niche it might be in the community – to rally others in support of the idea.

The way you communicate your idea to early adopters differs from how you'll share it with the rest of your community. When we get to the phase where you need to reach the majority of the community, it's crucial to have a clear message. And we'll talk about how you can articulate your story to achieve that goal later in the process.

But early adopters are primarily motivated by their attitudes and beliefs, which means you don't need a polished pitch at this stage. I always find it encouraging when naming early adopters because I can turn my perfectionist brain off for a bit. Early adopters are OK with some bumps in the road, disruptions, and wordy descriptions of your idea.

The rest of your community – listed as the majority and laggards – are motivated primarily by social pressure and understanding how your idea tangibly helps them overcome a barrier or problem they have. But with early adopters, you don't need to worry about that nearly as much. You can motivate them to support you mainly on the merit of the idea. This is where you can sell the dream without having to present a precise roadmap for how you'll realize it.

You'll come to discover the difference when talking with an early adopter versus a person in the majority. They respond to you differently. They'll ask different kinds of questions. Their eyes will sparkle when you share an innovative idea, even if it's still not fully developed. The more people you talk with, the more you'll see these differences.

Nancy Lee, a respected behavior change consultant and

professor at the University of Washington, describes her three different approaches to the three groups in the diffusion of innovation curve as "show me, help me, make me." For early adopters, you simply need to show them your vision, which as we'll discuss later, you can do with prototypes. For the majority, you need to help them understand the value of your efforts with clear messaging; for that, you'll need to articulate your story in a way that helps them overcome specific challenges. And for laggards, you often need to make them join you. But this isn't where you should put your energy now.

In the early going, you want to identify champions willing to work with you and constantly improve your idea. Early adopters are great at this. They can balance being super supportive of the original concept with providing valuable suggestions.

Your critical first few early adopters are your first followers. As Derek Sivers explains in his TED talk:

> *"It takes guts to be a first follower. You stand out and brave ridicule, yourself. Being a first follower is an under-appreciated form of leadership. The first follower transforms a lone nut into a leader. If the leader is the flint, the first follower is the spark that makes the fire."*

First followers provide the type of support that a parent might offer, combined with the constructive feedback of a coach. That's precisely what I got from Cindy, one of my favorite first followers.

———

I met Cindy during my couch-surfing days, while spending lots of time in our office. Not having a place of my own, I spent every free moment I had there. We had a Dunkin' Donuts right above us, and I came to know their staff quite well. The guy that worked the evening shift loved playing Brittney Spears on repeat, and unfortunately, our ceiling provided no buffer. You could hear it all, loud and clear. So if you worked in our office between the hours of 10 p.m. and 2 a.m., you were bound to have "Baby One More Time" stuck in your head. I came to think of that office as the perfect collision of coziness, creativity, and 90s pop music.

When you're starting your own organization, it's quite the adrenaline rush to have a news article written about you. I remember when the first journalist (not the same as a first follower, mind you) visited my office as I showed her around our new space. Unsure of her musical preferences, we made sure she didn't visit during the evening hours.

The next day I eagerly opened the newspaper, Onward State, to see what was written. This was the start of the article:

"Walking down the narrow, dimly lit steps ... and continuing through the door at the bottom, you take a minute to look around what is currently a work in progress. A wall across the room – painted so obnoxiously green that you are almost blinded – greets you immediately. A burnt-orange, crushed velvet sofa sits in the corner to your left, with a feel that uncomfortably reminds you of your grandmother's sofa, sending goose bumps racing up your arms. A retired picket fence, dismantled and stained a deep brown, hangs horizontally on the wall, adding color to an otherwise lifeless grey wall (an odd choice, compared to the screaming green wall across from it)."

Goosebumps! I suppose that was our goal – to give people an exciting feeling of possibility for our town. Regardless of what others thought, I loved that couch, and the office, which was essentially my home for nearly a year and a half. At least that's how I felt until I met Cindy.

I would describe Cindy as someone who is perfectly ordinary and utterly unique. She's a mom who volunteers at the senior centers around town and loves to hike. She knows every great watering hole and branch to swing on in the woods. She doesn't hold any special positions or sit on any fancy committees or boards. If you were in a bureaucracy, Cindy wouldn't make it on any list of influential people to contact or potential partners. That's not her. That's not how she makes an impact. Rather, Cindy simply follows her big heart and natural curiosity to see where they might lead.

She is the kind of person that randomly pops into places. That's her style. It's what makes her utterly unique. She has no problem putting herself in situations where her life intersects with yours. She followed her curiosity one day into our office and joined me on our burnt-orange couch to talk about what happens at New Leaf.

Some people you meet have a way of making you feel fully seen. That's Cindy's superpower. In that conversation, I was no longer the person behind New Leaf (as if I was synonymous with the organization itself); I was simply Spud. She reminded me that my worth lies entirely in myself, and never in the ideas I help to bring to life. In her gentle but direct way, she ended our conversation by asking, "So where do you sleep?"

"On couches," I replied. I explained that we were pursuing an alternative career path that didn't make much money, but that we loved the work and felt called to it; and that the lack of a comfortable bed was the least of our current concerns. Christian popped his head out from the 3-by-6-foot closet under a stairwell, which we had converted into his "private" office, to lend his agreement.

I could tell she didn't buy – or fully understand – my answer.

Twenty-four hours later, Cindy returned and told me I would be living with her from here on out – along with Christian. She declared the statement as if we had already agreed to it, rather than posing it as a possibility for us to consider.

She had a basement room that she would leave unlocked, and we were to move in right away. We shook on the agreement with one term: For our "rent," we had to play board games with Cindy once a week. She definitely didn't drive a hard bargain. That moment changed my life (and led to my obsession with collecting and playing board games).

I can confidently say that none of the ventures I have been fortunate enough to lead in State College would be possible without Cindy's support. I would have left town and felt burnt out had it not been for Cindy popping in unannounced.

Cindy was our first follower. And no matter how hard you look, you'll never find a reference to her contribution on any website or news article, and you won't see her posing for photos at any ribbon-cutting ceremony.

That's the thing with first followers. They often get overlooked. When you look at another community and are inspired by what they've been able to create, it's often hard to spot the hidden first followers who helped make them a reality. The leader (or lone nut) typically gets some recognition, along with the formal partners that like to see their name in the news, but rarely first followers.

I think that's why it can feel a bit discouraging when hearing about what other cities are doing because all we read about are the partnerships required to get the initiative off the ground. Building partnerships and funding projects to the tune of hundreds of thousands of dollars or more sounds intimidating. But the news reports often miss how those ideas actually emerge in the early days. Partners like recognition, and often expect this when they lend their support.

But Cindy helped us with no other expectation than that we would play Settlers of Catan and Ticket to Ride with her every week. That's how first followers work. They aren't in it for the publicity. They are in it because their internal compass and belief system compels them to provide support in whatever way they can. By the time partners get on board, first followers have often moved on to uncovering the next idea to rally behind and support.

Your goal in this step is to find your Cindy. When you do, make sure that person knows just how grateful you are because their role is so significant.

I lived in Cindy's basement for over two years, coming and going late into the night. We'd tiptoe through the backyard and into the backdoor, trying not to wake her neighbors. I came to realize that I wasn't the only one who had benefited from Cindy's generosity. She had hosted countless other people in that basement space. It was a resource she had, and she chose to use it for the betterment of the town.

That's the fantastic thing about first followers. They often have offbeat or even bizarre resources that you can't plan for or might not even know you need. They're the type of people that make custom slides on the weekends.

Cindy taught me more about community building than most

books or experts on the topic. She taught me to be curious and unafraid to pop in for a visit with people in your community. She taught me not to be concerned with titles or committees or recognition. She taught me to confidently declare good ideas to others, just as she had suggested living in her basement. And she taught me the value of bartering and trading whatever creative resources and skills you have at your disposal in the early days when building momentum around your idea.

Leveraging those assets is the quickest way to build momentum organically and from the ground up. To discover those unplanned and untraditional offers of support, you have to be willing to put yourself out there and start talking to people.

When we launched New Leaf 2.0, Cindy was there helping us hang our cardboard office from the rafters. When we needed fancy centerpieces for upcoming events, she would hike to hidden spots in the woods where she collected unique rocks to place candles in. When we kicked off Educate 20/20, she was the only person over the age of 40 to jump on the RV with us for a portion of the trip.

First followers will lend some of the most genuine and authentic support in the critical early days of your idea. That support comes entirely from the effort you invest in them by building relationships, not partnerships.

On Educate 20/20, we were fortunate to meet with Seth Godin for an interview. The rest of us were slightly intimidated and excited to interview such a well-known thought leader. But Cindy didn't know who Seth was. As a result, Cindy didn't try to put on a good face around him. She was simply her authentic self.

At the end of the interview, she got up and started clapping because she was so moved by what he said. The rest of us were trying to play it cool. We didn't want to mess up the audio file by having distracting noise in the background – or let Seth know how much we admired him. But Cindy was doing what she does best, genuinely being a first follower and getting behind any good idea she came across.

Find your Cindy. Because to build momentum, you need your first follower. You need someone willing to stand up and applaud your idea unashamedly.

CHAPTER 3.2

STAGGER INCREMENTAL ASKS

SO HOW DO YOU GO about finding Cindys? And how do you frame an invitation that makes it more likely for someone to say yes and offer their support?

To start, it's important to realize that this is about inviting that person into a community. You're asking that they actively contribute. This is what's called a participatory community.

In talking about creative community building, it's essential to understand that communities provide a sense of belonging at their core. That's the short and sweet of it. There's lots of academic literature and nuance you can dive into if you'd like. Communities often foster companionship, shared understanding (language, governance, skills) and a common identity (values, experiences, artifacts). But ultimately communities help people find belonging through a shared interest.

"The opposite of belonging is fitting in," as Brené Brown wisely notes. For so much of our lives, we float from group to group trying to fit in. We bend, compromise, and adapt to the norms, values, and rituals of those around us. But when we stumble across true belonging, we no longer have to force ourselves to fit in. We can simply show up as our whole selves. Brown goes on to share:

> *"As it turns out, men and women who have the deepest sense of true belonging are people who also have the courage to stand alone when called to do that. They are willing to maintain their integrity and risk disconnection in order to stand up for what they believe in."*

Think of the lone nut and first follower. They each had immense courage.

As a community builder, your goal is to create a project, idea, or initiative that others can stand behind because they believe in it.

Communities vary in so many ways. But for our purposes, let's categorize them as either passive or dynamic.

Passive communities are groups where you can find belonging, without needing to contribute extensively. There are lots of examples of passive communities, from Harry Potter fans to mountain biking enthusiasts. Passive communities form naturally around shared interests. They don't require anything from a community builder to help them grow and evolve.

Dynamic communities, on the other end of the spectrum, are comprised of active members. These consist of groups of people gathered around a shared interest while moving in a strategic direction together. As Seth Godin writes,

> *"Dynamic communities realize they can harness their collective intelligence to achieve something together, in addition to simply belonging."*

Harry Potter fans evolve into dynamic communities when they start organizing their own Quidditch tournaments or create a Wizard Activist School to train new community builders. (Yes, this is a real thing run by a group called the Harry Potter Alliance.) Similarly, when mountain biking enthusiasts begin working together to build new trails for beginning riders or host gatherings to encourage more female riders to join the sport, they are becoming a dynamic community.

What transforms passive communities into dynamic communities is the degree to which their members are able and motivated to work toward a common goal. At its core, that's what makes a community participatory.

Community builders secure this kind of participation by asking for it strategically as part of their work. In short, that involves staggering incremental asks of their members.

There arc lots of different ways to invite participation. I use a simple tool called the community commitment curve.

As time goes on, you should offer more opportunities for people who've taken an active interest to engage. You might start by asking someone to volunteer for one hour or to review a logo you designed. You could invite that person to lunch or ask him or her to read a particular news article.

The point is to focus on bite-size actions that make it easy for participants to commit.

With each action, your role as a leader is to be thinking about what ask comes next. That doesn't mean someone has to keep saying yes to everything, but as a community builder, you're giving people the opportunity to increase their participation over time.

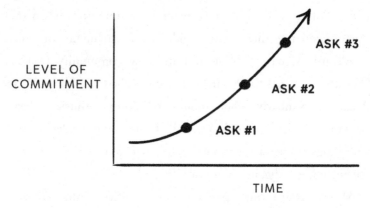

LEVEL OF COMMITMENT

ASK #1

ASK #2

ASK #3

TIME

A community commitment curve illustrates how to stagger varying levels of commitment between your asks.

It's easy to forget to follow up with the next ask. It's also a mistake to expect new volunteers to tackle an overly demanding task at the outset. The important thing is to ease into participation. In this way, ineffective asks are much like being asked to meet the in-laws on a first date; you can't rush into a relationship!

Think of the difference between being asked to sign a petition versus attending a city council meeting and speaking in front of a crowd. You can't start by inviting someone to speak on behalf of your cause publicly. But you also shouldn't stop offering opportunities to participate after you have someone sign a petition.

The entire focus of New Leaf for the first few years was to help people take the first step to make radical change in the world. But we knew it was a lot to ask someone to join a project, let alone pitch a project immediately. So we found ways to incrementally get them more engaged in our work, ultimately leading them to get actively involved in a project. Our commitment curve looked similar to this:

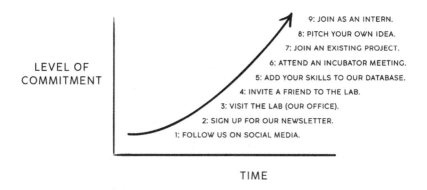

LEVEL OF
COMMITMENT

9: JOIN AS AN INTERN.
8: PITCH YOUR OWN IDEA.
7: JOIN AN EXISTING PROJECT.
6: ATTEND AN INCUBATOR MEETING.
5: ADD YOUR SKILLS TO OUR DATABASE.
4: INVITE A FRIEND TO THE LAB.
3: VISIT THE LAB (OUR OFFICE).
2: SIGN UP FOR OUR NEWSLETTER.
1: FOLLOW US ON SOCIAL MEDIA.

TIME

Not all of the asks were relevant for each person, but our goal was to create ways for folks to continually get more deeply involved in our work. Sometimes we would add new asks, like building cardboard furniture or decorating our office for the holidays.

It was well-known that we routinely had 50-plus interns, each designing their own internships because we expected them to shape their own experiences. There was no boss, managers, or paid staff; and you wouldn't find an organizational hierarchy chart anywhere near our office. We were empowering people to join and participate in a decentralized fashion.

Ori Brafman writes about decentralized organizations in his

book "The Starfish and the Spider: The Unstoppable Power of Leaderless Organizations":

> *"In a decentralized organization, there's no clear leader, no hierarchy, and no headquarters. If and when a leader does emerge, that person has little power over others. The best that person can do to influence people is to lead by example."*

For those on the outside watching us from within their centralized bureaucracies, it must have looked like chaos. They had no way of understanding what we were doing and who was in charge. We didn't micromanage, and it likely looked like anarchy to outsiders. But for those of us on the inside, it was nothing more than early adopters becoming increasingly engaged in the work. There was a clear pathway to get incrementally more involved.

As the founders of the organization, my partners and I saw our role as portraying a compelling vision of what the future could look like, and establishing trust and friendship with anyone who wanted to join us to create that future. We didn't know it at the time, but researchers had found that these qualities are critical when rallying followers around an idea.

From 2005 to 2008, Gallup studied 10,000 followers to determine what people want from a leader. They found that "when followers trust their leaders, one in two are engaged. When followers don't find leaders trustworthy, only one in 12 are engaged at work." Even more importantly, they found that portraying a hopeful vision of the future was one of the strongest indicators for why someone chooses to follow. Sixty-nine percent of those who strongly agreed that their leaders made them "feel enthusiastic about the future" were engaged. By comparison, only 1% of those studied who disagreed with the statement were engaged.

By the end of our first year, we had found ways to catalyze one to two projects per month with a completely decentralized group of teams. Our model was counterintuitive to many, but in a town that routinely stifled innovation, we seemed to be producing results.

The more people got excited about being involved in a group that actively got things done, the more they participated and the more they invited their friends to join. That's how participatory communities grow. Small asks today lead to sustained engagement tomorrow.

One of my favorite examples of participatory communities – which specifically leaned on early adopters – is CreateHere in Chattanooga, Tennessee. Started in 2007, the concept was simple: Invite a bunch of young creatives to the region and encourage them to create. Those who participated received a stipend and could start a public art project, build a dance studio, or create an incubator for new businesses. The only stipulation was that they were expected to create something.

The simplicity of the program is what made it so successful. There weren't any stringent expectations or processes participants had to follow. They simply had to identify the unique way they wanted to contribute and actively participate in the town.

Eighty fellows participated in the program over five years, and toward the end, they began advertising their "Supernova" to the community. Signs were posted on bus stops and business windows counting down the number of days to the explosive end of the organization that had supported all of their projects. That's how CreateHere was designed from the beginning. The organizers never wanted the innovations that emerged from the program to get stuck in an organization, so they planned on killing the very thing that supported their creation.

Participants in the fellowship knew that if they wanted to sustain their work, they would have to form collaborative relationships with others in the community. CreateHere gave them the space to experiment and try things with no expectations of what needed to happen to their creations. But if they wanted it to be more than a fun experiment and to continue what they started, it was up to them, not the organization. They empowered their members to have autonomy in deciding how they wanted their projects to grow.

Today, countless organizations throughout Chattanooga owe their start to the CreateHere initiative. Not all ideas survived. A dance studio was shuttered. Other projects, like the placemaking ventures, learned they were actually in danger of gentrifying the area. They transformed their work into a new project called Glass House Collective, an amazing group of artists and designers working in concert with the community to animate their neighborhood. And some projects scaled up and took on new funding, like co.starters, which has found ways to support entrepreneurship ecosystems locally and around the world.

CreateHere was a public call to recruit innovators to come and play in their town. The program likely didn't make sense to a lot of the community, but early adopters instantly recognized it for what it was: an innovation that they were eager to get behind as a fellow or supporter. As a result, Chattanooga is now home to some of the most thriving creative communities, with active participants co-designing their town. Participatory community has been baked into the cultural fabric of the region.

———————

As your idea grows into a project and others start supporting you, it can be tempting to replicate what big organizations do. We naturally assume we need to create staffing hierarchies, write grant proposals, or start having regular, formal meetings. But at this stage, what you really need to do is focus on engaging people, which encourages creativity.

Gallup research found that "engaged employees are ten times more likely than actively disengaged employees to strongly agree that they can take creative risks at work."

I enjoy creating these opportunities for others by working outside of the system, designing my own initiatives free from many constraints. But my wife, Katie, excels at building creative communities within existing organizations. It doesn't matter whether you work from within or outside a system, you need change agents on both sides in order to create a lasting impact.

In the early part of our relationship, Katie founded a program called Stand for State, an initiative within Penn State University that taught people how to intervene in potentially risky situations and create a more inclusive campus. The program launched from the bottom-up after gaining support from a handful of first followers within the university. Soon after, the effort had spread to 20-plus Penn State campuses across the state.

With Stand for State, Katie worked with early adopters that were invested in these issues and identified a different, but complimentary and collaborative approach to the current work that was already being done to address sexual assault, relationship violence, and acts of bias on campus.

One of the first steps she took was to build a community commitment curve and map out ways to meet students where they were. In order to help people see themselves as active bystanders capable of making a difference in their community, she needed to start with much smaller asks and had to find ways to creatively empower students and staff to show up as their best self. They needed to see themselves as people that step in when it counts and stop someone from getting hurt. Her solution: Fill a room with 2,500 balloons.

During the launch week for the initiative, she filled a prominent glass-walled room in the center of campus with green balloons. Inspired by a violence prevention strategy called Green Dot, each balloon represented one small positive act someone can proactively take to counteract a risky situation. Katie asked her early adopters to hang out in the middle of it all. That was the first ask on her community commitment curve: Simply get people to step into the glowing green balloon-filled room. It was impossible not to walk by and ask what was going on. Soon after, a steady stream of people were flowing into the space.

Once they were engaged, the early adopters were able to strike up a conversation. Large silver balloons floated around the room with prompts that got them thinking about what a safe campus for everyone would actually look and feel like. This allowed them to follow up with the next ask on the curve, which was to invite them to take one proactive step to make that dream a reality. They could send a text to check in on a friend they were concerned about, learn more about patterns of relationship violence, or bring up the need for discussing these topics in their student club meeting. The goal was to demonstrate that intervening as a bystander is a proactive choice, not always a reactive one, and that everyone had a role to play in creating a safer and more inclusive community.

The approach was a success, and word about Stand for State spread. Another action week was held with the same commitment curve approach, and by the end of that week, Katie and her team of volunteers had tracked more than 13,000 individual proactive steps taken across the community. The key was that she started with a small ask that met people where they were and then incrementally helped folks see themselves as active participants in the movement. In doing so, she recruited more and more people along the diffusion of innovation curve to get involved.

Three years after the initiative launched, 36% of the 47,000 students at the main campus were able to articulate the steps to intervene, and 56% of students recognized their brand. More significantly, students that had heard of Stand for State (they didn't even have to attend a program, which was a bigger ask on the commitment curve), were significantly more likely to recognize that bias, relationship violence, and sexual assault were issues on campus, and most importantly, that they had the agency and influence to do something to address those issues.

While making incremental asks, your goal is to create scenarios where your early adopters begin to see themselves in the story that is being co-created. Naturally, in time, they will intrinsically feel more motivated to contribute beyond your initial ask and recruit others to join them.

———

Nearly a decade after starting New Leaf, I found myself working on another creative venture in town, 3 Dots. As an arts and innovation center, we knew the importance of inviting community members to see themselves in the unfolding story and frequently found ways to show others how to collaborate with us.

Drawing inspiration from Harry Potter, we decided to create our own interactive, talking portraits. As an art gallery, we were used to having lots of framed pieces on our walls.

But what if we could frame the budding community builders in our town, the folks who were forming their own dynamic communities? Would their stories – their triumphs and failed attempts – draw people to our space and inspire them to pursue their own ideas? Normal, everyday people were making their mark and shaping the future of our community, and we wanted to bring their stories to life.

So we got to work and embedded computer monitors on the wall, covering the tangle of wires and electronics with planks of wood. We placed empty picture frames around the monitors and then took photos and videos of members of our community who were active participants in our town.

As a visitor walked up to the wall, one picture frame would suddenly come to life. The person in the portrait would wave, introduce themselves, and proceed to tell the visitor about a project they were working on in town. The framed person would start virtually walking around between the other picture frames as they told their story.

With our community commitment curve in mind, we wanted to captivate the imagination of every visitor who engaged the wall and stumbled into our downtown space. The point was to encourage all who visited to consider what they had to contribute to their community and find out how to get started.

Rather than featuring the work of famous painters, we showcased our neighbors, specifically those who had transformed an interest they had into a dynamic community. We featured folks passionate about local food who created an Iron Chef-inspired cooking competition for local chefs at our farmers markets. We showcased individuals who cared about racial justice and created book clubs and podcasts for women of color to openly share about their experience living in our predominantly white community. These were people who were rolling up their sleeves and making their mark on our town.

After each interactive picture frame came to life, those watching were encouraged to share their own idea with our organization or find a way to get involved in the project described. As you seek participation, challenge yourself to find ways to capture the imagination of people who are thinking of joining you. Don't get stuck thinking that your initial asks need to be dulled down to ensure people get involved. You can have a simple prompt for participation packaged in a whimsical form like our talking picture frames or a room full of balloons.

Every time I walk past that wall of faces, I am reminded of the importance of investing in and leaning into the relationships within your social network. The projects that last and ultimately create a sustained impact in a community often emerge from the culmination of lots of tiny asks and acts.

BUILD MOMENTUM THROUGH TRUST

SO, YOU'VE GOT THIS IDEA and have identified a few others who are also passionate about it. Now, you might be wondering, what can you do to get the ball rolling? How do you generate momentum?

If you're not sure, that's normal. Some people are natural connectors and organizers, whereas others prefer to be the idea person or focus on operations. As Malcolm Gladwell writes in "The Tipping Point: How Little Things Can Make a Big Difference":

> *"Look at the world around you. It may seem like an immovable, implacable place. It is not. With the slightest push – in just the right place – it can be tipped."*

The push you need to build momentum comes from early adopters. Regardless of your personality, you can find ways to enlist them to engage others for you.

Once you've identified someone willing to stand behind you, look at their network and find a first follower in their crowd. Not every early adopter will create a wave of momentum in their wake. Over time, however, you'll find that a tipping point emerges.

You need to be strategic with the relationships you are nurturing. It's about more than finding a random group of people to get behind your idea. You need to be intentional in engaging supporters to get their help in building a larger community.

There's no exact science for how you should scaffold support. It all comes down to knowing which early adopters influence other early adopters. This is an incredibly relational and fluid part of the process.

People like to be involved with projects that involve their friends and other people they respect. Early adopters like to be seen as having discovered those communities, and they naturally want to share what they found with those around them.

Ideas spread most quickly through trusted peers. It's the difference between getting a movie recommendation from a friend versus going online to search for ideas of what to watch this weekend.

A 2015 study by Nielsen found that 83% of consumers say they "completely or somewhat trust the recommendations of friends and family." Word-of-mouth endorsements from people we know and trust are the most reliable way to spread an idea – easily eclipsing news articles, websites, or ads.

Les Robinson, a community change consultant for

Changeology, writes about the importance of relying on trust in spreading innovations:

"[T]he adoption of new products or behaviors involves the management of risk and uncertainty. It's usually only people we personally know and trust – and who we know have successfully adopted the innovation themselves – who can give us credible reassurances that our attempts to change won't result in embarrassment, humiliation, financial loss, or wasted time.

"Early adopters are the exception to this rule. They are on the lookout for advantages and tend to see the risks as low because they are financially more secure, more personally confident, and better informed about the particular product or behavior. Often they will grasp at innovations on the basis of no more than a well-worded news article. The rest of the population, however, see higher risks in change, and therefore require assurance from trusted peers that an innovation is doable and provides genuine benefits.

"As an innovation spreads from early adopters to majority audiences, face-to-face communication therefore becomes more essential to the decision to adopt."

As I looked around at my community when launching Trailhead, I started to identify people I could potentially rally and tried to predict the influence they might have in different parts of our town. When I realized that my community didn't need physical trailheads, I immediately pivoted to finding guides and supporters.

I needed early adopters.

Because I had built some trust in the community by this point, I packaged my initial ask as a financial donation for this project.

I created a simple Google doc with a one-page description of what we were building. We were going to design a physical space for people to discover the great things about our region. Anyone would be able to drop in and meet with our guides whenever they'd like. Then each month, we were going to give the community $1,000 to launch cool projects. You could think of it as a clubhouse for local creatives.

The $1,000 grants weren't my idea. I found another community was doing this, and it was an idea that was made to be shared. Community builders routinely encourage and support each other in adapting and applying solutions that worked in one place to another community. Unlike other industries – where ideas are protected under lock and key and with expensive patents and trademarks – community building is largely open-source. Replicating a model from another town is one of the best ways to pay respect to those who forged a new path.

I was inspired by the Awesome Foundation, which exists in cities worldwide and consists of 10 friends each giving $100 per month. With those pooled funds, they give out no-strings-attached $1,000 grants to anyone with an awesome idea. Anyone can apply for a grant or start an Awesome Foundation chapter in their town. It's the perfect example of a largely decentralized organization with no fancy hoops to jump through or rigid approval processes.

So I made my ask to early adopters clear. If you give $100 per month, you'll be a part of deciding which awesome grants we give out, and you'll get a key to our clubhouse for local creatives.

I made the first ask to two close friends of mine, Christian and Jared. Christian was my business partner on multiple ventures, and Jared had been a fellow collaborator in many of those organizations. We went on a hike, and I shared my vision. They quickly committed. So I put their name and photos on the second page of the Google doc.

I then reached out to some of their friends who they recommended I chat with as well. They pointed me to Matt, a local designer and foodie; Jason, a well-known musician who was their neighbor; and Dana, a friend who organized dance groups in town. Upon reaching out to them, they all responded similarly that, essentially, if Christian and Jared were in, they were too. Now we had five supporters on the Google doc.

I asked this new group who some of their mentors in town were that I could contact. They suggested some well-known local leaders and entrepreneurs, including a professional photographer, a 3D-printing expert, and the head of a local craft studio. I reached out to each of them, explained who else was involved by sharing the Google doc, and they all had a similar response: "Well, if everyone else is in, I'm in too!" From there, I reached out to their friends who were the chief editor of the local newspaper, the director of our chamber of commerce, and the CEO of a local bank, who said roughly the same thing and committed to join us as well.

Soon we had the head of our local community foundation, borough council representatives, founders of improv groups, and the lead for our large entrepreneurship incubator. We were forming quite the crew of creative changemakers, and it was all because people they respected and were friends with had said yes before them. (It was amazing how much easier this was than trying to induct them into a secret society.)

I was hosting the Potluck Brainstorms around this time, so I would talk to a few more people each month. I'd show them the Google doc of who else was involved and steadily we grew our team, from the bravest first followers to our curious early adopters.

One of the most powerful ways to grow momentum is to lean into the trust established by others long before you. If you are unsure where to start, simply ask your supporters for three people they would suggest talking to next.

Once we had a critical mass of more than 30 people, I then went back and built the organization. That's what everyone didn't know. At that time, we didn't even have a space where their coveted key would work; doors were opening, sure, but there wasn't yet a physical one to unlock. I hadn't officially reached out to the Awesome Foundation. I had no idea how much rent would cost downtown. But now that we had our team of early adopters, I was confident I could at least pursue those questions and my vision.

This may seem backward, or inverted, compared with how most people build organizations. The traditional process involves spending a significant amount of time creating pitch decks, business plans, and strategic priorities. The fledgling organization (or the idea of an organization) develops in a fancy incubator. The entrepreneurs seek approval from the leaders of their town, or bounce their idea around once a month in a committee. They spend much of their time building the shell of an organization, and the people come later.

Ground-up community building works in reverse. It's far more effective to build participatory communities by rallying people who share a common desire or intention, and then creating the shell of an organization around those people. You might miss this distinction if you're not involved directly, but it's a critical difference.

It took us more than a year before we could find a space, and during that time, our organization continued to evolve. We worked with a fiscal sponsor for the first year, so we weren't distracted by having to create a nonprofit organization. A fiscal sponsor lets you collect tax-deductible donations through your partner without needing to create your own nonprofit.

We built prototypes of our work and added more partners to strengthen the plan and ensure we could sustain the momentum we'd gained from those early adopters. Eventually, Trailhead became known as 3 Dots, the arts and innovation hub in State College.

It would have looked a lot cleaner on paper had we designed 3 Dots from Day One, found the funding, and opened our space. For folks looking at our town from afar, that's probably the narrative one might expect for how this community space emerged. But that's not how community innovation works, especially bottom-up innovation.

Innovation ebbs and flows, ideas grow and change, and you have to stay nimble and attuned to the community's needs. Had it not been for piggy-backing on the relationships of those first followers, we would never have been able to build 3 Dots into what it is today. Trust was the critical variable that allowed us to build momentum.

In 2014, the Google Civic Innovation Team began to explore a group of people known as Interested Bystanders. These were people who were aware of the issues in their community, but were not acting on them. The Google team found that 49% of Americans fell into this category – knowledgeable about what's going on and yet not getting involved.

In 2018, the Knight Foundation continued to build upon their research to explore what it takes to get nearly half of the country more involved in their community. They found that "lack of trust is a major barrier to making civic life more meaningful and inclusive." This is particularly amplified in minority communities.

As Google explored what it would take to encourage Interested Bystanders to participate more fully in the community, it found that "friends and family are the most influential to Interested Bystanders' civic participation." Google coined the term Civic Broker to describe the role that community members can play to encourage their friends to be active participants alongside them.

As a community builder, this is an important finding. Nearly half of your community are people who are interested in local issues, but need a nudge from a friend to get involved. By leveraging the trust you have established in your social networks, as a civic broker, you can quickly build momentum around your idea and encourage others to follow you.

The Knight Foundation found that for civic brokers to be most effective, they should focus on people's interests or passions around issues in their community. This is what motivates many people to get engaged where they live. Once you've identified a cause that people care about, you can leverage your social capital to encourage them to participate. The researchers observed that "through meaningful, trusting relationships, civic brokers help interested bystanders engage by navigating a complex civic landscape."

As I assembled my early adopters, I focused on individuals

I knew cared about making our town a vibrant and creative place. In addition to name-dropping people who they trusted, I tapped into their specific interests. When I talked with our local chamber of commerce, I explained how this would contribute to a more robust economy. When I spoke with business leaders, I explained how this would make it easier for them to recruit potential employees to move to our town. When I talked with the head of our newspaper, I explained how this would generate more positive stories in our community.

Not to be confused with manipulation, framing your offer and value proposition differently for different people recognizes the varying needs and interests of those in your community. Demonstrating this win-win perspective is an appropriate way to speak to the potential for your vision.

By the time we opened our doors at 3 Dots, we had already given out a dozen $1,000 grants, garnered numerous media mentions, and had hundreds of community members eager to volunteer, paint, and host events. We had tons of people we'd already engaged with on our community commitment curve, and as a result, they were deeply invested and planned to continue their involvement.

Because our early adopters were involved in so many well-known organizations around town – local banks, newspapers, chambers, and government – the broader community was excited to get involved. That's the magic of early adopters; they allow you to build a wide network of support and participation without having to secure formal partnerships with groups.

As you begin compiling the names of those in your network who can help you build your idea, don't worry about frustrating some people or getting turned down by others along the way. There were many people with whom I shared my Google doc of faces who said no; simply, they didn't fully share the vision. And that's OK.

Your goal is not to win everyone over, but to find the early adopters.

Early adopters are only one-sixth of the diffusion of innovation curve. So for every one person you talk with who is excited to get behind your work, expect five to say no and call you crazy (at least in the early going). The more no's you get, the more quickly you'll reach as many people as you need to who say yes.

One of my favorite stories on this comes from a colleague, Scott Sherman, who leads an organization called Transformative Action Institute. He shares the following with the students he coaches:

> *"Risking failure is the best way to overcome your fears. Most of us don't take risks because we are afraid of failure, and fearful of rejection. Ironically, the best way to defeat your fears is to confront them directly.*

> *"There is a true story about a man who wanted to ask out a female acquaintance, but he was too timid and shy. He was afraid that she would reject him. He was afraid of looking foolish. He was afraid of destroying the friendship. In a nutshell, he was simply afraid of failure.*

> *"He went to a psychiatrist who told him that she could help him overcome his fears, but that he would need to do whatever she said. 'Are you really serious about overcoming this problem?'*

she asked him. 'If so, you must follow the advice that I give you.' He insisted that he would do anything to overcome his fear of failure.

"'Then I want you to collect as many rejections as possible in the next month,' the woman said. 'I want you to get rejected 75 times in the coming weeks. Your goal is to collect as many failures as possible. I will give you a nice way to approach women diplomatically and politely, so that you don't appear like some stalker or psychotic guy. But then your agenda is for the women to reject you again and again and again.'

"Of course, there was rich psychological insight in her advice. First of all, the man would soon learn to overcome his fear of asking women out. He would get used to the bitter sting of rejection; he would even look forward to it, because, after all, his goal was precisely to get rejected. Soon it would be much easier for him to ask women out, and he would be immune to the fear.

"Second of all, he would find that he wouldn't get rejected all the time. His fears turned out to be unfounded. Yes, many women turned him down, but an equal number agreed to have coffee with him and go out on dates. He ended up failing in his attempts to get rejected. He soon gave up the game, because he had overcome his fear, and had gained much greater self-confidence."

We consider rejection to be a bad thing. But if the fear of failing or looking silly is preventing you from talking to people, reframe your goal. Rather than try to assemble a team of five people who say yes to support you, make it a goal to get 25 no's. When our goal becomes to fail, we take the pressure off ourselves and, in the process, accidentally succeed along the way.

Naming early adopters is all about getting outside of your comfort zone to ask people to follow and support you. You'll be surprised how many people will say yes when you simply make the ask.

STEP 4

VISUALIZE
A PROTOTYPE

I WAS UPSTAIRS WHEN I heard the shriek.

It was one of those screams with a defining pitch and personality to it that could only indicate one thing: bees.

I came rushing down the stairs – skipping every other step as if launched from a slingshot – and as I turned the corner, the scene in front of me was unlike any I had imagined. This was the exact opposite of what you wanted to see in your dining room.

When you develop a prototype, you expect things to go wrong. You build something, based on what you've envisioned, and inevitably, it breaks. You're not meant to have it all figured out yet, and the primary goal is to learn from this step, not to sell a finished product.

That's fortunate, because had we sold what we were still developing, we would have found ourselves on the business end of a lawsuit.

In 2013, we launched the co.space, a 20-person intentional community for young changemakers. Tenants live together in a creative home and build community while supporting one another's visions for change. Imagine merging the authentic community you find at a summer campground with the creativity you find in a Google office. It's one thing to talk about changing the world, it's another to get 20 people to all do their dishes.

Intentional communities stretch you, provide a team to support your adventures into the unknown, and teach you how to compromise with 19 other people. And that is made exponentially more difficult when one of your housemates has a love for bees.

Each month, we came together as a house for our Pitch Dinner. We all went around the table as we ate and pitched an idea to the house that we wanted to pursue. Some pitches were to the point, while others involved elaborate props and theatrics. By the end of the meal, we voted, and the winner received $100 to build a prototype of their idea in the house.

We've built indoor rock climbing walls, podcast recording studios, little free libraries carved out of fallen trees, and cave showers with stalactites above your head, all for $100. But one idea has since gone down in co.space history: the indoor beehive.

The pitch was simple: If we had a beehive at the co.space, we could support declining bee populations, harvest our own honey, and learn about the importance of local pollinators. But instead of an outdoor beehive, the tenants pitching the idea envisioned sitting down to dinner and watching the bees build their hive as it hung on the wall beside us. That twist – to have the beehive inside the home – captivated me and others living in the house. We excitedly gave them $100.

With the seed funding secured, a few of the tenants worked together each night in our basement workshop to build a beehive that could hang indoors.

The design was pretty slick. Made in the shape of a hexagon, the hive could expand as the colony grew in much the same way the honeycomb structure expands inside an actual hive. A clear tube that ran from the hive and through the window let bees enter and exit as they pleased. The prototype was soon complete, and our housemates were eager to show us what they'd built.

We hung it proudly in the center of the dining room and waited for the bees to arrive. As it turns out, when you order bees, they arrive in a shoebox. Or at least that's what it looked like to me when I came upon a neatly packaged brick of 10,000 bees sitting on our doorstep one morning.

Their arrival naturally created a buzz in the house, and we all watched with rapt attention as the bees were placed inside the "beecosystem." The team was equally excited to use this moment to unveil the name they'd given their indoor beehive.

Then we waited.

Of course, we'd spent a lot of time leading to this moment, searching online for pointers on how to create a beehive. But we hadn't come across any other examples of people building an indoor beehive. So we weren't quite sure what to expect next.

But as the hours passed, the bees seemed to acclimate to their new home. They soon began flying in and out through the plastic tube, collecting pollen in the neighborhood.

I spent most mornings eating breakfast while watching the bees construct their home with intricate care, doing their special butt-wiggle dance to communicate to the others where they had found pollen. I daydreamed about the co.space having a butt-wiggle dance routine of our own – you know, to signal to others in the house when we found a new ice cream shop or gyro stand in town.

The beecosystem quickly became the focal point of the house, and our hive grew surprisingly fast. Soon, we were nearing 40,000 bees – all separated by a thin piece of plexiglass mounted inside a wooden frame. But no one ever paid much attention to the tube that went into the window – until the shriek.

Coming to the bottom of the stairs, I saw one of our tenants cowering in the corner of the room. Overhead, thousands of bees swarmed. They formed a large mass that ebbed and flowed, like an ocean wave cresting just below our dining room ceiling. The buzz was deafening, and the bees dropped what looked to be pollen, or poo, on my helpless housemate.

It's one of those moments you don't prepare for as a landlord. I wondered what my lawyer would say about this one.

With little idea of what to do, I called the tenants who built the hive. I assumed they had a contingency plan in case of this kind of emergency. They didn't. So they rushed home and we all huddled on the other side of the house, assessing what to do next.

It turns out that, in affixing the tube the bees used as their entryway and exit, the team that had built the hive had used the wrong type of glue. It was the kind that, inconveniently, didn't adhere to both wood and plastic – the kind of glue you should avoid when building an indoor beehive made of wood and plastic. Because of this glue goof, the tube going through the window had slipped out of the hive, and the bees flew freely into the house.

But that's the point of a prototype.

Prototypes teach you something. They aren't meant to work smoothly. They are intended to be tested and rapidly iterated upon. As things fall apart, you learn and improve for the next round. The team eventually solved their glue problem. It just took the tube popping out a few more times to verify which adhesive worked best.

In the time since, the team has traveled the world, participating in a variety of incubator programs from San Juan, Puerto Rico to Santiago, Chile, while building an actual business around the beecosystem. Their globe-trotting social impact journey all started with a $100 bet to build a prototype and see how people would react.

———

Creating and visualizing a prototype is one of the steps I find people most often skip. It's also one of my favorite steps.

We would never have built the momentum we needed to launch New Leaf had we not tangibly showcased our idea with the cardboard mock-up. Nearly every venture or project I've undertaken since has been captured in cardboard while developing the concept. We built a cardboard version of what would eventually become 3 Dots on my ping-pong table during the final Potluck Brainstorm. We had Play-Doh and Legos that people could use to add their suggestions to the evolving blueprint. Once we got the keys to 3 Dots, I asked a friend to find as many cardboard boxes as he could. Soon, we were building huge cardboard walls – 12 feet tall and higher – around the space and had a cardboard stage and furniture we moved around to provide different perspectives.

Cardboard mock-ups may not be your prototype of choice. But

don't let the material stop you. Your main goal is to create something you can show others that invites them into an experience.

We've all heard the advice around the holidays to give people experiences, not more stuff. Experiences are more memorable. We won't soon forget bees escaping inside the house, or even sitting for breakfast, watching the bees do their special dance. The experience is what remains with us, less so the tangible product or thing we created.

Keeping that in mind, when creating a prototype, you should:

1. Show, don't tell.

2. Weave in wonder.

3. Divide big ideas by 500.

CHAPTER 4.1

SHOW, DON'T TELL

PROTOTYPES HELP YOU DISCOVER THE range of what's possible within your town. You could study a book of zoning regulations or put something on the sidewalks and see how folks respond. That was our goal when we built the P-Funk Mothership.

The Mothership is one of the most iconic stage props from the 1970s. It was a fixture at many Parliament/Funkadelic concerts. A group of rotating musicians, P-Funk was iconic in the African American community. Their concerts were always over the top, full of color and energy. One of the quintessential parts of their show, for a time, came in the closing moments when the Mothership – a large spaceship with strobe lights and fog machines – descended on stage carrying the musical collective's lead singer, George Clinton (also known as Dr. Funkenstein).

I had never heard of the Mothership until I went down to the National Museum of African American History and Culture in D.C. On the top floor of the museum, proudly displayed as the centerpiece of the collection, sits the Mothership. It's quite an impressive piece, but I'll be honest, I was already sold when I heard fog machine.

Once we launched 3 Dots, we began hosting the Potluck Brainstorms there. At one of these events, we were discussing ways we could reinvigorate our downtown through creative placemaking. Placemaking is the art of letting communities co-create their towns and creatively strengthen their public spaces. It's about making communities where people are excited to live, work, learn, and play and takes on many forms – from public murals to swings at a bus stop to pop-up art galleries in back alleys.

As the facilitator, I had everyone attending write random nouns and objects on slips of paper that they put in a hat. For one of the rounds, I challenged them to pick a single noun out of the hat, find a partner, and develop a creative solution that would combine each of their nouns into a placemaking initiative. The majority of the ideas were not great, as we anticipated. But every now and then, a gem emerged.

As participants were frantically creating as many pairs as they could in the 20 minutes allocated, the director of our Downtown Improvement District approached me. He told me he would prefer to observe rather than get involved (a response that I've sadly heard time and time again from people in positions of power). We both sat there watching the chaos emerging around us.

Toward the end of the process, I had everyone pause and look at the wall of sticky note ideas they had generated. There were at least 100 ideas posted. I encouraged them to scan the wall and see if any had potential. They had 20 minutes in small groups to convert the creative ideas into a few tangible placemaking projects we could implement in one month with minimal resources. I challenged them to find a way to create spaces of transformation in our community.

We gathered as a group for the final debriefing, and there was one idea that generated the most excitement: the Mothership.

Two participants had combined the nouns "funk" and "cardboard." Without much thought, they wrote on their sticky note the idea of building a cardboard replica of the P-Funk Mothership while hosting a giant dance party on the street. They shared their vision of having a spaceship downtown, complete with lights and fog machines, hovering over the sidewalk.

As they pitched their vision, the head of the Downtown Improvement District whispered in my ear: "This is fun to watch, but no one will ever implement these things. My experience tells me this isn't remotely possible."

Doing all I could to bite my lip, I listened with one ear to a voice from the top-down explaining how this was not possible. With the other ear, I listened to voices from the bottom-up, sharing their excitement for what they saw emerging. I held the tension as the new and chaotic creativity collided with rigid order and bureaucracy.

These two approaches frequently butt heads. Chaos is where new ideas emerge; it is the place where artists thrive and kids play. Order allows organizations to survive; it is where management exists and projects find structure and support. The problem is that order often slides further into control and micromanagement. City leaders are often too quick to explore why an idea is unlikely to work or start identifying all of the hoops one would need to jump through.

The beauty of a prototype is that it allows you to continuously iterate and navigate the space that lies in between chaos and order – the chaordic path. This path strikes a balance between convergent and divergent thinking and allows new ideas to take flight and be sustained. I often use this framework to introduce innovation into a community that's constrained by bureaucracy and "this is how we've always done it" thinking.

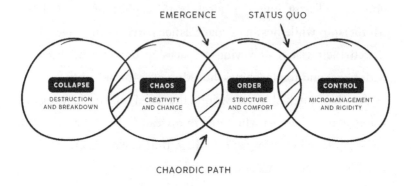

The chaordic path is where new ideas and innovation thrives.

In a study conducted by Adobe, they found that 75% of people do not feel they live up to their creative potential. When they explored what was inhibiting people's creativity, they found institutions – like schools and businesses – are often the culprits. The reason is that these institutions too heavily prioritize a need for order and control. Eighty percent of those polled reported feeling increased pressure to be productive rather than creative at work. This kind of pressure can undermine your efforts to launch a creative initiative in your community.

The director was skeptical of the Mothership idea because he had seen how rules and regulations had killed similar ideas in the past. It's not that he's not supportive of a thriving downtown; he's been one of the more helpful collaborators over the years. But he's been conditioned to think there is only one way to get new ideas through – that it would need to be reviewed by committees and approved by zoning, that red tape was inevitable.

We were going to show him a different path. That path required building a prototype of the concept to demonstrate what was possible. But we weren't about to start with a formal pitch to the borough council to host an outdoor dance party with a flying spaceship. We were just going to build a prototype. Much like the New Leaf cardboard party, we needed to quickly and cheaply show what was possible.

We got right to work putting the call out to our community to help us build said spaceship. We set a time and place and told people that anyone could help. The town was intrigued.

We collected piles of cardboard, rolls of aluminum foil, and a stack of lumber. We had no blueprints or idea of how to build a spaceship. All we had to work from were a few pictures we'd found online showing what the actual P-Funk Mothership looked like on stage. We were learning by doing. As my father always jokes, "Measure once, cut twice."

As new people arrived to help, we would pass the baton to rotate who was in charge throughout the day. One person would lead the design for an hour or two and then someone else would take over. Few people had actual construction experience, and this was definitely not up to code. But after a few hours, we had a 10-foot-wide spaceship that lit up and emitted fog out of its rocket booster feet.

Conveniently, someone added shoulder straps to it so you could wear the 100-pound spaceship and walk around town with it. That's certainly not a design element I would have thought to include, but that's what happens when you source the wisdom of the crowd: the end result is always better than, or at least creatively different from, what you'd imagined. You may initially find it difficult to release your creative control in this way. If this is your inclination, trust in the ability of your community and resist your desire to control the outcome and micromanage your vision.

Now we just needed a party. We picked a day and spot on the sidewalk and went looking for DJs. Sure enough, one called back who had DJ'd for the Jonas Brothers at a giant concert venue the weekend before. He needed something different for the upcoming weekend. It didn't take much convincing to explain to him that we were about as different as you could imagine. He was in!

A lighting designer joined our movement, along with our local dance community, and soon enough, a proper dance party was forming on our sidewalk. It was impossible not to stare at us as we walked the spaceship down the sidewalk and mounted it to a railing. I'm sure there was a zoning regulation preventing you from chaining your bike to that railing, but I was willing to take a bet that there were no regulations for spaceships. I've always thrived in that gray space.

Our only challenge was that we picked a sidewalk with lots of street lights. We needed it to be dark for our spaceship to have the proper effect. So I got a tall ladder, a roll of black trash bags, climbed the light posts, and covered them with trash bags. I'm sure that was against code and would not have flown had we pitched it to the borough council.

The cardboard spaceship was placed right alongside the sidewalk, which caused quite the stir. Passersby encountered a DJ and lighting designer on the upper patio and someone dancing with a glowing hula hoop in the bushes along the sidewalk. As they approached, we invited them to join our dance party. We danced the night away in silly hats, which we handed out to anyone who appeared to take what we were doing too seriously.

That evening, our street corner was popping! Lights were flashing off buildings, funk music was filling the alleys, and pedestrians were drawn into the impromptu dance party. Older adults, college students, homeless community members and young kids all joined in on the fun. I only wish the director of the Downtown Improvement District had been there.

But we had shown what was possible. We tested boundaries and gave the community hope for what our downtown could look like. And the cops never once asked us why we blacked out the street lights.

Now I'm not advocating recklessly flouting rules. But I am encouraging you to loosen constraints that keep you from launching a prototype. When you have an idea, don't automatically assume you have to go through formal channels to bring it to life. There are often simpler and more direct paths.

A well-known urban planner and former mayor of Curitiba, Brazil, Jaime Lerner, describes that approach this way:

> *"The lack of resources is no longer an excuse not to act. The idea that action should only be taken after all the answers and the resources have been found is a sure recipe for paralysis. The*

planning of a city is a process that allows for corrections; it is supremely arrogant to believe that planning can be done only after every possible variable has been controlled."

Ultimately, our Mothership replica was disassembled and repurposed into something else. The experience taught others in our community that they can approach their town in ways they hadn't considered before – in playful and pop-up ways. Not everything you create has to be a permanent installation. And yet, these pop-up experiments often lead to long-lasting efforts.

One of my favorite organizations that do an incredible job of helping people reimagine their communities is Better Block. The nonprofit focuses on assisting neighborhoods in leveraging prototypes as a way to show what's possible in their communities, a concept known as "tactical urbanism." I met Jason Roberts, who runs the Dallas-based group, in Toronto, Canada, as part of a fellowship program focused on designing creative communities. There, he shared a story about a prototype that was little more than toilet plungers to demonstrate the power of imagination in helping communities discover what's possible.

Over the past few years, without any forewarning, cities across the U.S. woke up to find toilet plungers glued to the sides of their streets. But what might appear to be an act of vandalism had a more significant purpose: highlighting the importance of divided bike lanes. Rather than make a presentation to city planners, the individuals responsible for the toilet plunger bike lanes chose this memorable demonstration to make their point.

Residents discovered a divided bike lane that they assumed

had been properly installed by the city. Naturally, they started using it. Bikers immediately felt safer commuting, and no one – other than city officials – questioned how it emerged. Bikers and motorists didn't even realize that they were zipping by toilet plungers, assuming instead they were fancy dividers created for just this purpose.

Eventually, the plungers were removed – sometimes by the city and other times mysteriously in the middle of the night – because you can't have toilet plungers glued to your road. But the idea often sticks, or at least stretches the bounds of what's possible.

Jason has helped numerous communities create similar pop-up experiences involving temporary bike lanes that resulted in permanent bike lanes being built. His team has even created an open-source solution, Wikiblock, that allows any community to easily build their own prototypes. The Wikiblock website has free designs that you can download to build your own benches, bike racks, and bus stops. All that's needed are a couple sheets of plywood and a laser cutter, which can often be found in community makerspaces. Without even glue or nails, you can quickly assemble life-size Lego-style designs and form everything from outdoor stages to pop-up street vendor booths.

Creating opportunities for your community to engage in playful prototypes helps strengthen your project and your town. From 2008 to 2010, the Knight Foundation and Gallup teamed up to explore what makes people love where they live and why that matters. They studied 26 cities and polled more than 43,000 residents. The results were surprising.

Typically, towns assume people choose to live where they do because of job opportunities, the local economy, or perhaps the safety record of a community. But this report found people feel most attached and committed to their community because of three variables: social offerings, openness, and aesthetics. The researchers describe these variables in the following way:

- **Social offerings**: Places for people to meet each other and the feeling that people in the community care about one another.

- **Openness**: How welcoming the community is to different types of people, including families with young children, minorities, and talented college graduates.

- **Aesthetics**: The physical beauty of the community, including the availability of parks and green spaces.

The towns where people felt most attached to their community because of what it offered in these three areas had the highest gross domestic product, or GDP.

In other words, the more opportunities people had to connect and beautify their communities, the better that town performed economically. The research results were consistent for small towns such as Macon, Georgia and big cities like Miami.

Putting toilet plungers on the road or hosting pop-up dance parties around a cardboard spaceship may not seem super strategic initially. But these kinds of activities lead residents to feel more attached to their communities.

As you think about your community intervention, what boundaries do you think need to be tested? What experience could you create that would stretch your community's imagination? How can you create an opportunity for others to feel more attached to your work and the wider community?

A 2018 poll by the Pew Research Center found that 4 in 10 Americans don't feel attached at all to their communities, and only 16% felt very attached. In line with the diffusion of innovation, there is a significant proportion of your community that has the potential to deepen their engagement. The poll found that "social connections are also linked to community attachment. Adults who say they know all or most of their neighbors are more than twice as likely as those who don't know any of their neighbors to say they feel very or somewhat attached to their community (77% vs. 32%)."

Creating prototypes is simply an artistic way to invite your community to connect face-to-face around a shared experience and deepen their engagement. In doing so, those individuals will begin to feel more attached to their community thanks to the efforts you're leading. Research has shown that those who participate in artistic and cultural activities are more likely to be civically engaged in their communities.

If you hope to rally support around your idea, you don't need to start with a polished pitch. Instead, you should kick things off with an experiential event. Set aside any perfectionist tendencies and create something your community can experience and that you can learn from. There's a wise proverb that says:

"I hear and I forget; I see and I remember; I do and I understand."

Our cardboard spaceship wasn't perfectly made. There were lots of elements that needed work. The fog machines were attached with ropes that knocked into your legs when you strapped into the spaceship and carried it around. The whole thing was most definitely not weatherproof. Screws were poking through various boards because we lost the box of shorter fasteners while building.

But that's OK. We learned. We pivoted. We adapted to the feedback we continuously received from our community and used those insights for future interventions. Throughout the process, we created a small moment of delight and possibility for our town.

CHAPTER 4.2

WEAVE IN WONDER

ONE OF MY FAVORITE BOOKS that dives into creating memorable experiences is "The Power of Moments: Why Certain Experiences Have Extraordinary Impact" by brothers Chip and Dan Heath. One of the stories that has most inspired my creative prototyping is about a red telephone.

They recount the story of an old hotel in Los Angeles. It's nothing special, built in the 1950s with few renovations made over the years. The beds are average and the wallpaper is outdated. At first glance, there seems to be no reason travelers would go out of their way to stay there. And yet, it's one of the highest-rated hotels in L.A. on Tripadvisor. Why? It all comes down to that red telephone.

Out at the pool, there's a red telephone – the kind that has a curly cord and a shiny plastic veneer – with a simple sign hanging above it reading "Popsicle Hotline."

If you pick up the telephone, an operator on the other side promptly answers and asks what kind of popsicle you would like. You pick your flavor, and soon enough, a staffer with white gloves and a silver tray delivers your popsicle free of charge to you beside the pool. And just like that, what may seem like a relatively average hotel etches a spot in your brain thanks to that popsicle delivery and other memorable amenities.

When I'm trying to visualize a prototype for my community, I always ask myself: How can I create a moment worth remembering? And what do I hope to learn as a result?

When I put a ball pit on the sidewalk and hopped in, it caused people to pause. I learned about the changes my fellow State College residents wanted to see in their community.

A lifesize cardboard mock-up of a coworking space invites people to role play, and it taught me what amenities we'd need to include for someone to pay for a membership at New Leaf.

When people hear the phrase prototype, it's easy to assume you have to physically build something, like a beehive. And unless you're the tinkering type, that can sound intimidating.

But prototypes are fundamentally about experiences. To create an experience, you don't need a big budget, an elaborate plan, or lots of supplies. You don't need to build a giant spaceship with fog machines (although no one is stopping you). All that's required is some creativity.

———

Many years ago, I traveled to Amsterdam to meet a friend who told me I needed to experience an alternative way of building community. Facilitators from Brazil were invited to work in a small, marginalized community that was home to many refugees and immigrants. Their goal by the end of the week was to create an oasis. That meant transforming an otherwise overlooked and underappreciated part of the neighborhood into a vibrant community gathering spot. And they were going to do all this with no money.

The group is called the Elos Institute, and they have been organizing these community-led transformations, which they called the Oasis game, for many years throughout Brazil. This was one of the first times they brought their practice to Europe to see how it would be received in a new cultural context. I didn't want to miss out, so I booked my ticket to the Netherlands.

Early on in the process, the facilitators blindfolded members of the team and dropped them off in the community. (At last, I found my opportunity to join a secret society!) It was not exactly how you'd expect to start a project, but nothing about the Oasis game felt normal.

As the blindfolded participants stumbled through the streets, the first thing that naturally began to happen is that kids emerged. Children can't help but follow their curiosity, so naturally, they asked the blindfolded people what they were doing.

The volunteers responded by telling the kids that they were working on a project to create a magical oasis in the community and would love it if the kids would help. Since they were blindfolded, they asked the kids to lead them around and explain what they love about their community. The kids took the adults' hands and guided them, showing them their world from the unique vantage point of a child.

They tell them about the hole in a fence they like to hide

behind when they play tag. They explain where their friends live and which house gives out the best cold treats on a hot summer day. They take them to the pile of old tires that they use to build forts and to sand pits where they play.

The kids never seemed to ask the volunteers why they're blindfolded. They're just excited to show an adult their world and explain it to them in vivid detail.

This was how the Oasis game began. They called it the "appreciative gaze," and the goal was to identify hidden gems and pockets of the community that could be converted into participatory community spaces. Kids have incredible imaginations, so they can often envision things before adults can. By blindfolding the volunteers, everyone learned to see their community with fresh eyes as they kicked off the week-long experience.

The rest of the game was guided by four simple rules. In their book "Walk Out Walk On," Margaret Wheatley and Deborah Frieze describe the rules of the Oasis game laid out by its founder:

1. Whatever we build has to be simple, accessible, and easy.

2. It can't cost anything. Whatever tools and materials we might need, we'll have to find a way to obtain without paying for them.

3. The product has to be something that we create collectively and with our hands. (It can't be an idea.)

4. It has to meet a real need in the community, as defined by the community.

Following the blindfold exercise, community members and volunteers rallied together to pick an area of the neighborhood to transform into an oasis.

I teamed up with groups building flower and herb gardens from the pile of tires. We painted murals on walls and transformed vacant patches of grass into soccer fields. We did all this with no money. The community rallied together. Residents donated resources, time, and energy. The community worked with whatever was contributed to the center. At the end of the weekend, they celebrated with a giant party and cookout. Neighbors emerged from their homes to join in celebration of what they had created together.

It was a beautiful example of what participatory community design looks like, and it all started with blindfolding volunteers. I didn't realize the importance of this initially, but their approach was incorporated into the program's name. This was a game, and games are experiences shared with friends.

Too often, community building involves consultants, policy briefs, and Excel sheets. It's just no fun. Games, by contrast, engage us, which is precisely what's needed to improve our communities. As Wheatley and Frieze note:

"Games are universal. There isn't a culture on Earth that hasn't developed traditions for teaching people how to create, imagine, and build, how to play roles and make believe, how to test our physical, mental, and emotional limitations. Games transform the landscape of our environment: a familiar room is now a castle, an abandoned square becomes a battlefield. We play games because they're fun, not because we're trying to be realistic, practical, or efficient. Games invite us to let go of our resignation and our sense of limitation – and simply to start dreaming, creating, and imagining."

Prototypes are your chance in the community building process to introduce laughter and play as you create something alongside your neighbors. I left the Netherlands inspired by what I participated in and committed to creating similar experiences in my own community. I've found there are plenty of ways you can make community building fun and engaging while still achieving your objectives.

You can hand out disposable cameras and ask community members to take pictures of the parts of their town they most appreciate. You can create a fake newspaper of the future with stories about what your town could look like if specific projects were completed. You can coordinate a flash mob in a part of your town that you want to transform, to draw attention to its unseen potential. We once created a fake holiday called "Take Your Parents to Work Day" when we realized it was hard for adults to understand what we were building. That was our prototype.

Whatever you choose, your goal is to create a moment worth remembering that teaches you about specific aspects of your community.

So how do you weave in wonder? How do you design for memorable and meaningful experiences?

One of the most important roles of a community builder is to create the conditions where others can dream about what's possible. In this sense, your role is much closer to that of a Disney Imagineer than a city planner.

In "The Power of Moments," Chip and Dan Heath write, "Defining moments can be consciously created. You can be the architect of moments that matter."

Memorable moments often involve wonder. Think about those rare moments when you find yourself completely in awe of the wonders around you. I think about when I got to swim with bioluminescent plankton at my wedding in Mexico, and when I stood beneath the vibrant Milky Way galaxy in the middle of the Serengeti.

Beauty inspires wonder when it so effortlessly takes our breath away and holds our gaze. Sheer scale, too, can provoke wonder, as we come to appreciate our role, purpose, and place in the world. Sometimes that scale reminds us of our significance, and other times our insignificance. Even the element of surprise can generate awe when our preconceived notions of the world encounter new realities or unexpected ways of living. Wonder is a dose of what's possible in the midst of what is.

So how do you create that feeling for others? We were intent on determining that as we set out to design the co.space. How do we create a home of wonder and possibility for those who would live there?

When you think of the moments of wonder you've experienced, how often have you planned for them? Had you actively sought this type of inspiration?

Typically, wonder sneaks up on us (though we can learn to be more receptive to it). It's that pleasant surprise that we encounter when we are open to receiving it and are present in the moment. If we live our lives at a hurried pace without ever taking time to pause and notice all that's around us, we easily miss potential moments of wonder.

So when trying to create awe-inspiring experiences for others, your first step is to create something that causes folks to pause, slow down, and focus on the now. As they become more present, introduce something that encourages them to consider what's possible – for themselves, their community, and their future. Then once you've got them entertaining possibilities, invite them to participate in the experience.

Creating moments of wonder involves pause, possibility, and participation:

- Get people to pause by disrupting the norm.

- Show them what's possible through beauty, grandeur, or surprise.

- Invite them to participate in the experience.

Consider these three elements when designing for wonder.

As we began renovating the co.space, I knew I wanted to embed some of the principles I learned from the Oasis game. I wanted my community to get a sense of what's possible in an otherwise ordinary home.

When you enter one of the stairwells to the co.space, you find yourself staring up into a mining shaft. The walls are made of rough rock. Rickety boards appear to be all that's keeping the cave ceiling from falling down on you as specks of glitter on the rock catch the light from a dim bulb overhead.

Instead of mindlessly running up and down the stairs, guests can't help but pause and look around, wondering if those are gems hidden in the wall just beyond their reach. They make sure to hold on to the handrail tightly as they ascend the steep staircase, curious about what's ahead.

When they poke their head around the corner at the top of the stairs, they discover a shower with stalactites overhead, and gushing water cascading out of the showerhead. They've just entered our guest room.

Our cave stairwell invites a moment of pause and possibility. Visitors aren't used to seeing a cave inside a house, and they begin questioning the purpose of a home in the first place. Then, at the end of the stairwell, as they find themselves in our guest room, they are invited to participate in the community we are building at the co.space. We encourage them to join us for a meal, stay the night, or otherwise offer their mentorship to those in the home. We invite them to explore what is possible and be an active participant.

When we transformed the libraries into innovation labs, our first step was to rearrange all bookshelves, tables, and chairs. When students and teachers walked in, they knew something was different. For most, this moment of surprise invited them to pause and follow their curiosity to see what was going on. (Of course, I did have to console one librarian who found the change in routine to be too disruptive.)

But we didn't stop at rearranging the furniture. We unveiled our giant Pinterest board of possible design ideas, invited the students and teachers to give us feedback, and then handed them a crowbar to start ripping up the carpet.

A few days into the process, the superintendent approached me to share his experience. He'd received numerous calls from parents in the district asking him what he had done. They told him their kids came home with their hands bloodied and torn open, and yet, the students couldn't stop smiling and talking about their day at school. After the superintendent told parents what we were doing, they told him to keep it up; a few blisters were more than a fair trade for getting kids to fall in love with learning.

It was simple. We disrupted their norm and invited them to pause, had them reimagine what was possible at their school, and then gave them a chance to help build that dream.

Wonder begins with an element of surprise that breaks the script of everyday life. Chip and Dan Heath write in their book that a study examining hotel reviews on TripAdvisor found "when guests reported experiencing a 'delightful surprise,' an astonishing 94% of them expressed an unconditional willingness to recommend the hotel, compared with only 60% of guests who were 'very satisfied.' And 'very satisfied' is a high bar! Surprise matters."

We are called to do more than simply satisfy those in our community, which is too often the sole focus of city planning. When we design communities of delight and wonder, those who we serve are far more likely to get engaged and spread the word.

Nabeel Hamdi, a pioneer of participatory planning and author of "Small Change: About the Art of Practice and the Limits of Planning in Cities," discusses the importance of doing small prototypes to evoke a sense of wonder in one's work:

> *"In order to do something big, to think globally and act globally, one starts with something small and one starts where it*

counts. Practice, then, is about making the ordinary special and the special more widely accessible – expanding the boundaries of understanding and possibility with vision and common sense."

Our cave room has inspired many tenant-led additions to our home at the co.space. Our tenants have gotten really good at asking for forgiveness, rather than permission, when it comes to creating their own wonder.

One tenant asked me if she could build a Narnia closet in her room, to which I responded yes (although I had no idea what she meant). She instantly breathed a sigh of relief as she told me she had actually built it the previous weekend. Apparently, some of our rooms now have secret passageways that connect them through their closets. It's a hidden moment of wonder for future tenants to discover.

DIVIDE BIG IDEAS BY 500

I STUMBLED ACROSS ONE OF my favorite prototypes of all in the backcountry of Boulder, Colorado. Instead of cardboard, it was made almost entirely out of giant rubber bands.

I was in town visiting a group reimagining higher education who I'd met during Educate 20/20. The organization, called Watson Institute, trains young social entrepreneurs from around the world. One morning, I decided to get up early and hike the Flatirons – majestic rock formations shaped like their namesake – which rise from the edge of Boulder.

I hiked deep into the woods, and while others relied on detailed maps, I flipped a coin at each fork to decide where to turn next. I didn't have a fancy hydration backpack or trekking poles. I was clearly a casual East Coast hiker, and now found myself in the company of avid hikers. Hoping not to stand out for all the wrong reasons, I pressed ahead and soon found myself overlooking stunning vistas of the town below.

Continuing on, I came upon two hikers, the first people I had seen in quite some time, casually waiting alongside the trail. From a distance, I knew they were fancy Colorado hikers because they had some strange contraption on their legs.

I approached, they waved, and I could tell they wanted something. They asked if I had a few seconds to spare. There was no one else around for a half-mile, and unable to come up with an excuse to duck their request, I obliged.

They told me they were designing clothing to assist backcountry thru-hikers – essentially people who hike really long distances. The strange contraption on their legs wasn't something they purchased from an outdoors store in town; it turned out to be an elaborate prototype made of rubber bands.

Designed to attach over your pants, as you lifted your leg, the bands would assist, hopefully easing the strain on long hikes. It looked like a poorly constructed Iron Man suit made out of rubber bands and duct tape. Naturally, I loved it!

But I had to know: Why were they hanging out here? Don't get me wrong, the views were fantastic, but they surely were not talking with crowds of people. I had to be the only person they had seen in the last hour.

You, too, might think that waiting to survey people where there was next to no foot traffic didn't make any sense. But they told me that's exactly where they'd run into their target customer. They wanted feedback from backcountry thru-hikers. So to find them, they would regularly hike deep into the woods and sit along a trail waiting for hikers to pass.

When visualizing a prototype, we have to think about the people we want to serve. This step is about asking powerful probing questions to a target audience that's excited to build momentum around our idea. Ultimately, you want to get feedback from those who are most eager to help you bring your idea to life. As Tom Wujec, an innovation thought leader, explains: "Prototyping is the conversation you have with your ideas."

The problem is that many of us wait too long and get nervous showing our initial ideas with those outside our inner circle. A study by McKinsey & Company in 2018 followed 300 companies for five years to explore the business value of design and prototyping. They found that 60% of the companies they surveyed use prototypes too late in the process, and when they do share them, it is only within their internal teams. The most successful companies shared prototypes frequently and early on with outsiders, celebrating the multiple iterations of an idea.

Granted, the entrepreneurial hikers I encountered in Colorado could probably have gotten away with hanging out at an REI or Patagonia store to talk with hiking enthusiasts. But I respected the determination it took for them to do their market research deep in the woods.

As you consider your big idea, how can you create a prototype that is a fraction of the size, whether a tangible mock-up or an interactive experience, that allows others to see your vision? Who is your target audience, and how will you create a memorable moment to get them excited about your idea? You will get the best feedback from your neighbors when you show them, not tell them about, your idea.

A popular way to describe these efforts in the creative placemaking movement is 'lighter, quicker, cheaper" projects. Those are the three ways a prototype should look different from your idea's larger vision. By prioritizing solutions that require minimum resources and can be implemented within hours, you don't need to feel as attached to your work. You should be able to throw away a prototype without getting upset. Prototypes aren't meant to last; they are intended to teach and demonstrate.

It's for these reasons that you don't need comprehensive plans when implementing a prototype. Plans are helpful to launch large undertakings and projects. But for prototypes, it's expected that things won't go according to plan. So rather than spending time away from your community trying to create a plan, focus on simply being prepared. Come prepared to learn, adapt, and observe. This subtle change in approach – preparation over planning – can be especially helpful if you're someone who often gets stuck in the thinking phase and you find that you're unable to act on your ideas. Now, when you go off script – and you will – you'll be ready to adapt. Instead of worrying that you're not following a predetermined plan, you can nimbly move forward in whatever direction you need to go.

Our Pitch Dinners at the co.space were designed to teach folks how to create and visualize prototypes similar to that developed by my new hiking pals. We were inspired by a microgrant initiative we read about called Detroit SOUP. The project began in 2010 when a group of friends wanted to fund some small projects in their neighborhood. They met over a meal and dreamt up ways to help finance the projects, which would never make it on the radar of large funding agencies.

They invited their friends over and charged them $5 for a bowl of soup, salad, and a vote. While eating, neighbors pitched their ideas, and at the end of the night, all in attendance voted on who would get the pool of money. This was participatory by design, and everyone left invested in the success of the project they supported. The microgrants were small, often no more than $100, and were mainly designed to help someone take the first steps on an idea.

The co.space itself first emerged as a prototype. An older neighbor brought the idea to us. He casually strolled into our office, where a handful of young people were working, and confidently shared his vision.

Speaking to no one in particular, he asked not so rhetorically, "What if you all bought a house – a big house – and created a space similar to New Leaf, but for people to live in? My neighbors across the street are a fraternity, and they are selling their property. I think you should buy it."

Then he left. His work was done. He had sufficiently sparked the curiosity of every young person in that room. We were hooked. What would it look like if we bought a home? Nevermind that none of us had any money.

So almost immediately, we set about figuring out how we could buy a house. We assumed the first thing you need to do is assemble partners – that is, influential people with money and property and who make decisions like this regularly. We attended borough council meetings and redevelopment committees. We met with community foundations and talked with the university and real estate investors.

We tried for a year to find partners and failed. Only later did we come to appreciate that this is the last step in the process when building ideas from the ground up, not the first.

What we needed to do was follow our curiosity and ask probing questions. Then we could find our first followers and early adopters, and begin showing the town what the idea would look like in practice, through a prototype.

Getting curious was the easy part. We filmed a short video where we posed the question, "What if we bought a house and filled it with young changemakers?" We sent the video to as many people as we could, asking for their ideas and feedback. We collected ideas for making the programming dynamic, design suggestions for the house, and most importantly, the names of young people who'd want to live there.

We submitted our video to an online competition and got all of our friends to vote for it each day. We must have had a lot of friends (or relatives who took pity on us) because we won the competition and earned a place at a conference to pitch our idea. We ended up winning some cash, and now were able to showcase what was possible.

We got a hold of the RV we used for Educate 20/20, crammed 20 of us into it, and drove off to a cabin for the weekend. If we were going to create an intentional community for young changemakers, we needed to understand what that involved. We needed to live with lots of other people (rather than just in Cindy's basement).

We spent the weekend brainstorming how we would handle cooking and cleaning, and what projects we would tackle as a group. Then we put our plan into practice to see what worked and what didn't. At night, we bonded around a bonfire with aspirations of these connections lasting through to the following year. Of course, we still didn't have a house, but we moved forward as if we did.

One thing we decided during our weekend getaway was that we wanted to find local mentors. So when we came back, we rented out the lobby of a big house in town and invited community members to join us for dinner. We pretended the lobby was our house. In fact, we tried to figure out how we could buy the entire property from the owners, so we could actually live there, though ultimately, we weren't able to make that happen.

We called the night Mentor Meetup. We used the occasion to test what it would look like for tenants to meet local leaders over dinner. We had a big grid on the wall with photos taped up of everyone's faces. People could align two cut-out faces to indicate who they thought should have a conversation. This empowered the group to facilitate connections and become active, intentional participants in the community we hoped to create.

Our cabin excursion helped us test what we wanted to build among ourselves, and now the Mentor Meetup event gave community leaders an idea of what we were working on. We were slowly inching along the diffusion of innovation curve as we gathered more support.

At the Mentor Meetup event, we met future partners. That included our realtor and colleagues who knew of folks looking to sell the property that we ultimately purchased.

We spent a relatively small amount on prototypes to land a significant investment in our house. The cabin rental and Mentor Meetup events cost around $2,000, and soon we had a home appraised for $1 million. This was similar to how we spent $200 to create a cardboard mock-up of New Leaf that landed a $100,000 investment in the venture. Likewise, I spent $10 on a Christmas tree stand and cardboard prototype of the Innovation Trailheads after receiving a $5,000 fellowship stipend. When developing a prototype, divide your big idea by 500 to tangibly show others what you envision on a small scale and learn from their feedback.

By creating prototypes, you can prevent costly mistakes in the long run. That's something I wish I would have known back in high school when I built my first parade float.

I was always fascinated by the Macy's Thanksgiving Day Parade. It was a tradition in my family to have it playing on our TV every Thanksgiving. I would watch in amazement as the parade's over-the-top signature floats cruised through NYC.

When I was 16 and finally able to drive, I set out to build my own float. I signed up for one of the local parades and got to work. Having no idea what I was doing, creating a plan seemed silly. I couldn't find any blueprints online detailing how to build a float, so I decided to just wing it and see what happened.

I found a local farmer who let me use his barn and an idle 20-foot-long flatbed wagon. I bought a bunch of wood, chicken wire and tissue paper, and convinced my friends that hanging out in a barn every day after school would be fun. Somehow they bought it.

We transformed that barn into our secret clubhouse where we could tinker and experiment. We snuck a TV into the rafters of the barn and created a lounge out of hay bales. We plotted about all kinds of things as we looked down on the wagon below, and eventually, we landed on our theme. We were going to build a tissue paper circus.

We built tissue paper cannons (since I had to find a use for my fog machines), stretched a tightrope high above the scene between two poles, and placed our pride and joy in the center of the wagon: a 12-foot-tall, Ferris wheel with egg crates as bucket seats. We found an old motor at a Habitat for Humanity ReStore that we used to spin the giant wheel. We painted it bright red, yellow, and blue, and we seated our sibling's stuffed animals in the converted egg crates so that they could go for a ride. It was a glorious sight to behold.

As new ideas emerged, we found a space for them on the wagon. We bent chicken wire into all kinds of elaborate shapes and stuffed tissue paper into the tiny holes until our fingers bled.

Finally, we had a proper float. We unveiled it for its debut showing at the parade which consisted of small groups of kids and neighbors lining the street. We tossed candy and waved excitedly from the wagon bed. The day was a success. But after spending so much time behind closed doors building the float in secret, we were eager to let even more people see it.

The following day, we were asked to bring the parade float to my church to display for the congregation. Excited to showcase our labor of love for others in the community to see, I drove down to the barn on Sunday morning. My friends and I hooked up the wagon to our car, fluffed up the tissue paper, and made sure the float was in top form. After all these months, we were excited to reveal what we had been working on. The church was a five-minute drive away. What could go wrong? As I found out, a lot. For one thing, we never prepared for a highway overpass.

We soon discovered that when you drive on an overpass above a highway, you encounter wind – lots and lots of wind. Carved into the earth between towering trees, the highway created a giant wind tunnel. And if there's one thing you should never drive through a giant wind tunnel, it's a 12-foot tall Ferris wheel built by teenagers.

Hindsight being what it is (kind of useless), there's not much you can do when you see, in your rearview mirror, that a strong gust of wind has lifted your Ferris wheel into the air and forcefully dropped it on the other side of the road. As cars zipped by, the fabricated ride shattered into brightly colored shards of wood; teddy bears large and small were flung from their egg crates and scattered across the road. Frankly, it was a colorful and chaotic mess. The only saving grace was that the wind hadn't been blowing in the other direction, which would have launched the Ferris wheel off the overpass and sent it crashing down on the highway below. "Ferris Wheel Falls from Sky onto Car" was neither a news headline I wanted to be responsible for nor an insurance claim I wanted on my record.

A few simple prototypes or probes could have averted the costly disaster. We could have tested how windy the overpass was or how much force our Ferris wheel could withstand. Instead, we put all of our creative energy into building the giant float in secret, without outside input, and all it took was a single gust of wind to bring it crashing down.

Too often, we approach our ideas in the same way. We work on them behind closed doors, and try to polish them to perfection before they see the light of day. Rather than testing small versions of the idea daily in the real world, we wait until our projects are fully complete to show them off. And more often than not, a giant gust of wind knocks them down.

On the bright side, we learned a lot from the experience. The parade float inadvertently became a prototype for future community building efforts. We learned about big vehicles and wind, which was helpful for the Educate 20/20 road trip. We learned how to use chicken wire as a building material, which I later used to create our cave stairwell at the co.space. And what we remember most fondly from the whole experience was the epic failure. I largely forget the parade itself and all the time we spent building the float. But I can vividly call to mind the float taking flight and smashing into pieces on the road.

Prototypes, unlike your finished project, are meant to go wrong. When things go off course, you learn from them and are able to iterate. Ultimately, your goal is to improve, not prove, your idea.

Prototypes are nothing more than a first start. It's your crummy first draft, your back of the napkin sketch, your unpolished improvisation. A prototype is something that you rework as you go, a thought you're still formulating. It evolves, it grows, and eventually, you learn what's possible. As Tom and David Kelly, founders of IDEO, one of the world's leading design agencies, note: "If a picture is worth 1,000 words, a prototype is worth 1,000 meetings."

It's often best to be working on multiple prototypes simultaneously. By dividing your original idea into smaller versions, you can test out different variations and potential solutions without wasting loads of time and resources. After working with companies from around the world for more than two decades, researchers at IDEO looked back and found that "When teams iterate on five or more different solutions, they are 50% more likely to launch successfully."

Diversify your creativity and be willing to question your original ideas. If you have moments where you think the prototype you're building is silly or not fully thought out, you're on the right track. No one is expecting you to be a fancy consultant or policy expert with decades of experience. You're not developing top-down solutions. You're building from the bottom-up. Having a few holes in your prototype is only natural, and it allows the community to rally around what you're doing.

———

The point of building a prototype is to learn – to gauge your community's response and discover unexpected solutions.

When our bees flew into the co.space, we had to rebuild our hive. Unfortunately, sometimes our bees died. But more often than not, our hive split, and the bees thrived and then multiplied while we learned how to be better beekeepers.

We also learned about a creative way to deal with loud music. We had a neighbor who hosted large parties in their side yard, which faced our dining room, and it was always a challenge to get them to turn their music down.

But one day, with the help of our new pets, the problem seemed to solve itself. The vibrations from the heavy bass next door were enough to shake our buzzing friends into a frenzy. On cue, as all of our neighbor's friends arrived for their party, our bees defended their right to have a quiet home. If you've never seen 40,000 bees exiting a small plastic tube through a window, it's quite the spectacle.

The bees headed straight for our neighbors, who had disturbed their peace and quiet. To this day, I've never seen a bunch of college students run as fast as they did from that party. Cops busting an underage party couldn't generate that kind of panic. Our bees gathered in one of the large trees directly above the group, and once the party was sufficiently dead, they slowly returned to their hive. We got the peace we wanted without ever having to file a noise complaint.

Prototypes will always lead to new discoveries and insights that will help you move your project forward (or lead you to tackle a new one). You'll learn lessons big and small, like what type of glue to use. You'll also discover new problems that you may never have set out to address in the first place.

STEP 5

ARTICULATE YOUR STORY

BEFORE WE HAD A BEEHIVE, before we renovated and purchased a property, we had to recruit students to live at the co.space. Of all the ways we could have thought to articulate our story, we chose a chameleon car. It turned out that was a bad idea.

We had spent so much time to that point rallying early adopters for our ideas that we had never done a proper marketing or PR campaign.

We stumbled through our first few years trying things that we assumed would work, but they always ended up taking far too much time without really delivering results. We were great at telling our story to early adopters. But those same strategies don't work well when sharing a vision with the broader public.

That's why the next step in the CANVAS framework is all about learning how to articulate your story for that larger audience, those who aren't your initial cheerleaders.

In the early concept stages of the co.space, we talked a lot about how we envisioned having multiple homes worldwide, each reflecting the unique climate and culture of the city where they were located. We didn't want to replicate a cookie-cutter approach with our program and needed a way to convey that principle.

A moment of brilliance struck us, as aha moments always do, while visiting a pet store. What better mascot for our new venture than a chameleon! Chameleons adapt their color to the environment around them – the perfect metaphor for what we wanted to create. So we bought a pet chameleon.

His name was Pascal (we named him after the character in the animated movie 'Tangled'), and he hung out in the New Leaf office while we worked on the co.space project. It's hard not to be captivated by a chameleon, so he quickly became the talking point for those who dropped into our office.

Each time Pascal inevitably caught our visitors' interest, we used it as an opportunity to explain our vision for the co.space. It was a great way to rally early adopters in the first few months. We assumed a similar approach would work for getting the masses on board with our idea. We were wrong.

Pascal made an excellent mascot for our early adopters. But he was a lousy substitute for a compelling story that would reach a wider audience.

When it came time to recruit more people to apply to the home, we thought it was best to ramp up our chameleon marketing storyline. We knew we couldn't carry our pet around Penn State's campus to meet everyone. (Although we did try that for some on-campus events, drawing disapproving glances from university staff.) So we figured the next best idea was to build a chameleon car we could drive around to the dorms and classrooms.

We borrowed a recumbent tricycle from one of our friends – the kind you lay back in to peddle – built a PVC pipe frame around it, and covered the whole structure in a giant paper-mache chameleon. We painted our reptilian ride neon blue and its massive eyes bulged out from the bike, staring intently at passersby as it drove down the road.

We were able to ride the bike without anyone realizing that there was a person inside. You only needed to lift the chameleon's head to access the driver's seat. Once inside, you had to peek through tiny gaps on either side of the chameleon's eyes to see what was ahead. With limited vision, we did our best not to run into things or people. As we jerked and bumped our way down a sidewalk, many likely assumed the chameleon car was nothing more than a large remote control vehicle.

We provided no explanation on the outside of the vehicle regarding what it was supposed to be or why it existed. For the first few weeks, we forgot to put a sign on it with our logo. Our choice of color didn't exactly hit the mark, either. While chameleons can change to many different hues, blue isn't the first color most people associate with the lizard. So not only did the public not know it was a chameleon – most thought it was a strange lumpy dinosaur – they most definitely did not realize it was designed to recruit people to live in an exciting new co-living space.

That is, they didn't know this until a hand popped out the chameleon's side and, while startling people half to death, handed them a flyer. That was our marketing strategy. Ride around campus disguised as a giant chameleon and hand out flyers about a new intentional co-living space launching for young changemakers. It was as bad and as awesome of an idea as you are probably imagining.

We spent weeks driving around confusing onlookers. We snuck up behind people at bus stops, and rolled full speed down the main lawn as we spread the word about the home for creatives. We must have handed out over 10,000 flyers.

So, what – you might ask – was the payoff from our guerrilla marketing strategy? How many applicants did we get as a result of our bizarre ground game? If you guessed low, you might still have been too generous. For all our efforts, we received zero applications. Not one.

We may have got some exciting front page news coverage and felt 10 years younger while rolling around campus, but it didn't result in a single person applying to live at the co.space. That's because we didn't know how to articulate our story in a way that would allow us to reach the masses.

Fortunately, we learned from our experience, and so can you.

To spread the word about your idea and tell your story effectively, you'll want to apply three main concepts:

1. Invite others into a clear narrative.

2. Stand out.

3. Navigate the media landscape.

CHAPTER 5.1

INVITE OTHERS INTO A CLEAR NARRATIVE

FOR ALL THE FUN WE had riding around inside a giant chameleon, it didn't translate well into a clear narrative.

In the early days of the co.space, we were so focused on reaching first followers, that we forgot our goal was to create a message that was easy to understand so others could pass it along. First followers naturally want to recruit on your behalf, but you have to give them the tools to do so.

A blue chameleon car didn't quite cut it, and our original marketing language wasn't much help either. Our early messages often spoke about how cool the house was, and what you got through the included programming and retreats. We communicated through cute soundbites and taglines. We would use phrases like "the home for changemakers" or say that we help people "do life better, together."

But none of these messages spoke to the underlying need we were meeting. In time, we started to hone in on a message that was clear, compelling, and easy for folks to share with their friends. "We help you find the group of changemakers you've been looking to live with." In a nutshell, that's what we were about.

We help people who feel lonely or who have had crummy roommates find authentic friendships and connect with those who share a similar desire to create positive change in the world. Our message started to evolve as we began to listen to the themes emerging during our interviews with prospective applicants.

We often ask folks applying to the home what their biggest fear is. (That's in addition to asking what their favorite sound is and what they would do if universities didn't exist; we pride ourselves on conducting nontraditional interviews.) Time and again, applicants share with us that they are afraid of being alone – of time going by and having missed out on genuine friendships. They're not worried about solitude, but rather the kind of loneliness one experiences amidst a fast-paced culture that doesn't have time for deep connection and powerful conversations. Our community longed for transformative friendships. But rather than clearly telling that story and speaking to the need we were trying to help people meet, we obscured our message. The giant blue chameleon car disguised what we were all about.

As a community builder, once you've begun to identify a core need and solution worth pursuing (which emerges early on as you ask probing questions), your next step is to clarify your story. You want to do this in simple, direct terms that will connect with the masses, and eventually, partners. As Brené Brown puts it, "Clear is kind. Unclear is unkind." Never make people work to understand what you are creating.

Your message should make it clear what value your project provides and how people can participate. After all, a compelling story's purpose is essentially to help attract more people along the diffusion of innovation curve to join you.

One of the biggest traps that most community builders fall into (and I'm speaking from extensive experience here myself) is making the story's focus about themselves.

Let me say this so that my younger self can clearly hear it: You are not the hero of the story. Your project is not the hero of the story. The solution you've found is not the hero of the story. As long as your story centers itself on you and your idea – and not the people in your community – very few people will feel compelled to join you. Or they will feel compelled to participate for the wrong reasons.

The first few years, people wanted to live at the co.space because they got to live with Christian and me. We were some of the only young entrepreneurs in town working on social innovation. The fact that students wanted to live with us and benefit from our energy fed our ego, and we started to frame ourselves as the hero of the story.

But at some point, founders leave. When we evaluated most other co-living spaces around the world, many closed after a few years because they centered primarily around a charismatic leader or leaders. These types of co-living ventures would thrive for a few years, but once the original leaders moved on, the community fizzled. Not only did the financial model not allow for the community to continue, but the messaging that attracted folks to the home was not designed to last beyond the founder.

We didn't want to have that same problem.

As we removed ourselves from the message, people started joining the home because of something bigger than us.

It was never about how awesome the co.space was and how we had cool features like stalactites in our showers or rock climbing walls down our hallways. But when you ride a giant chameleon down the street without a clear message, you may as well tell people that. What we really wanted to do, however, was to speak to the very real challenge many students were facing, and how we could help them overcome it.

Of course, early adopters will think riding around in a blue chameleon is alluring, so you'll always have a dedicated crowd around you. It was never hard for me to find people who wanted to ride around campus handing out flyers in the chameleon car. It seemed like our storytelling strategy was working since people were so excited to ride the bike. But those first followers aren't the general public, who should be the entire focus of your message as you articulate your story.

To avoid making the same kind of mistake, try this simple strategy: Reframe your story so that instead of being the hero, you're now the guide. The hero of the story is your community – your target users, the people you ultimately want to serve and support. Your job, as a guide, is to speak directly to the problem they are experiencing and give them a simple plan to overcome that problem.

Think of any great story you've ever read; they all follow roughly the same framework. The main character encounters a problem. That person or animal or alien meets a guide who calls the character to action. The character embarks on a journey that helps him or her transform into the hero of the story. Then the character returns home to share their experience with others.

You are the guide, not the hero. You are Yoda, not Luke Skywalker or Princess Leia. Reframing yourself as the guide will help you clarify your message. Then you can present a simple plan that invites others to take action and join you.

Author Joseph Campbell popularized this concept through his framework, The Hero's Journey. In describing this narrative pattern, he shares insights on what a hero is bound to experience:

> "A hero ventures forth from the world of common day into a region of supernatural wonder: fabulous forces are there encountered and a decisive victory is won: The hero comes back from this mysterious adventure with the power to bestow boons on his fellow man."

Community building is nothing more than serving as a guide to beckon people on a journey. You're inviting them to step outside the "world of common day" and creating moments of wonder for them to experience what might be possible in their town. Psychologist Jerome Bruner famously studied the role storytelling plays when communicating and found that people are 22 times more likely to remember facts when they are wrapped in a story.

Numerous studies have explored why this is, and neuroscientists have found that when we are engaged in storytelling, our brain waves actually align between storyteller and listeners. Known as neural entrainment, scientists are discovering what we have known intuitively for centuries: that storytelling is one of the most effective ways to transfer our ideas to others, by causing our brains to sync up. This is why storytelling makes up two-thirds of our conversations, as noted by Jeremy Hsu in Scientific American.

There are four key elements that you should consider when articulating a story-driven narrative: (1) the hero, (2) the guide, (3) the plan, and (4) the future. Think of these elements as the Reader's Digest version of your key talking points for your project.

First, you need to describe the hero of your story who will be the specific community members you hope to serve. What do they want and what challenges are standing in their way? Next, position yourself as their guide. How can you convey empathy and authority when framing your message so that they trust you?

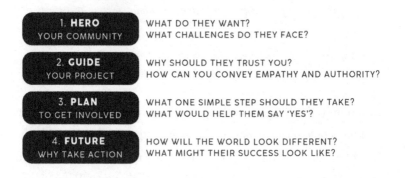

1. **HERO** YOUR COMMUNITY	WHAT DO THEY WANT? WHAT CHALLENGES DO THEY FACE?
2. **GUIDE** YOUR PROJECT	WHY SHOULD THEY TRUST YOU? HOW CAN YOU CONVEY EMPATHY AND AUTHORITY?
3. **PLAN** TO GET INVOLVED	WHAT ONE SIMPLE STEP SHOULD THEY TAKE? WHAT WOULD HELP THEM SAY 'YES'?
4. **FUTURE** WHY TAKE ACTION	HOW WILL THE WORLD LOOK DIFFERENT? WHAT MIGHT THEIR SUCCESS LOOK LIKE?

The four components of creating a story-driven narrative

Once they trust that you can help them overcome their challenges, then you are ready to share a plan for how the hero can take action. What simple steps should they take? What would help them say "yes" to joining you? Lastly, describe the future that awaits the hero if they were to take action. How will the world look different for them? What will their success look like? How is this different from their current reality?

When starting most ventures, I will often create a quick one-page document outlining these key story elements to help frame how I talk about the project with my community.

I first began applying story narrative to my work after reading about "StoryBrand" from Donald Miller. As Miller writes, "The story must always be focused on the hero, and if a storyteller (or business leader) forgets this, the audience will get confused about who the story is really about and they will lose interest. This is true in business, in politics, and even in your own family. People are looking for a guide to help them, not another hero."

In launching the co.space, I learned, by trial and error, lots of ways not to frame my message. So once we started 3 Dots, I crafted a more intentional and compelling story and invited the community into it from Day One.

The heroes in our story were local creatives who wanted to make our town an awesome place to call home. The problem they were facing was that they didn't know where to share their ideas and how to find like-minded individuals with whom they could collaborate. That's where we came in.

Our organization existed to connect, fund, and amplify their ideas. Our messaging focused on reminding them that they shouldn't feel disconnected, that their voice matters in shaping our town's future, and that we knew of others out there rolling up their sleeves and contributing to the cultural fabric of the region.

Then we presented a plan for them to participate. We made sure to end our messages with clear examples of ways people could get involved. Join an event. Host an event. Share your skill. Submit an idea for funding. Join as a donor. Volunteer to greet people at the front door. And if they took those actions, they would find the community they were searching for while helping to make our town an awesome place to call home.

There were lots of different calls-to-action that we could cue up depending on what we were focused on at the time. But the whole premise of 3 Dots was that the community would join in to take the next step – so much so that we baked the message directly into our brand.

The 3 Dots brand was built around the ellipses (...) because it was paramount that the community contributes to the evolving story of State College by helping to define our town's cultural identity. Our story was never finished. It was constantly being rewritten by those who came through our doors.

Some of the best stories end with a cliff-hanger. They invite you to consider what might have happened to the main character or how it could lead to future sequels. Great community-led projects do the same. They summon the community to wonder what their town would look like if they got involved. As Walt Whitman famously said: "The powerful play goes on, and you may contribute a verse."

Although you want to tell a compelling story, you also want your message to be an open invitation for your community to write the rest of the story themselves. In participatory communities, ideas live on beyond the founder.

———————

Stories are some of the most valuable components of any community. Yet, it's easy to make the mistake of thinking that things like money, property, donations, staff, or intellectual property are the commodities worth pursuing as a community builder. None of that matters if stories aren't handled with care and respect. As poet Muriel Rukeyser writes, "The universe is made of stories, not of atoms."

A colleague of mine, Cornetta Lane-Smith, ran a project called Pedal to Porch, which I have found to be an inspiring example of how to elevate the stories of those your project seeks to serve. Her idea was quite simple. We are all familiar with TED Talks and may often share them with friends around topics that inspire us. But rarely do we know the people on stage. What if you could unearth similarly powerful stories, but in your own community? These would be stories told by people you regularly have dinner with or see around town. That was Cornetta's idea, and so Pedal to Porch was born.

Cornetta would regularly organize groups of community members to gather on their bikes. Over a few hours, they would bike to neighbors' homes and listen to them give TED-style talks from their front porch. These were deeply personal stories based on the local wisdom in their neighborhood.

The project facilitated connections between neighbors and challenged the traditional narratives that shape a community. As the guide, she encouraged people to step into their own hero's journey and discover how they could meaningfully contribute to the town around them.

With our message clear at 3 Dots, the next step was to invite the community to join us for a design session. Before our renovations began, we wanted them to lend their voice and tell us what they wanted the physical space to look like.

Similar to the library transformation project, we could have easily come in and designed a dynamic and modern space. Our team had the expertise to do just that without outside input. But in doing so, we would have made ourselves the hero of the story. The community needed to design the space so that it centered the story on their experience, ideas, and contributions.

We put a callout in our newspapers, on the radio, and through social media inviting anyone to sign up for a 60-minute design charrette, a collaborative meeting where we talked through design ideas. Each event was capped at 24 people, and we hosted seven sessions throughout the week.

People arrived to 3,000 square feet of largely vacant space. Cardboard boxes and folding chairs were all we had to work with for furniture, and we had to sidestep odds and ends left behind by the previous tenant. In the center of the room, we set up a wall that we covered with hundreds of brightly colored aspirational images we'd found online showing the range of what we could do with our space.

So that everyone could see what we were working with, we kicked off the event with a quick tour of the building. I then gathered everyone in a circle around the photo wall. I shared the basics of what we envisioned happening within these four walls: 3 Dots was designed to be a community-led arts and innovation center that connects, funds, and amplifies the efforts of local creatives.

We then handed everyone a few stickers to vote on their favorite photos on the board. They were instructed to select images that struck them or inspired them. Once they'd voted, they formed small groups and spent time walking around the space together. They came up with a list of descriptive words for the space they envisioned, ways it could be used, and events they imagined could occur here. Then we reconvened as a group, discussed our ideas, and took note of the photos that had received the most votes. We talked about what all this might mean for how we designed the space.

After a week of repeating this process with more than 150 people, we held a party in the space to reveal two strong design themes that had emerged. The community wanted our space to serve as both a blank slate (a space of possibility) and a colorful palette (a space of wonder). The photos that received the most votes provided a template for how we could achieve this, and underneath those, we wrote a description of the activities people envisioned happening here. By the end of the evening, everyone could see their contributions embedded in the design direction, and were eager to grab rollers and paint the walls.

Whenever I facilitate a process like this with the community, I take into consideration three phases: the invitation, the hosting, and the harvest.

Phases to consider when facilitating participatory events.

The invitation is all about presenting a compelling reason why someone would want to show up and contribute their ideas. Imagine being asked to attend a party with no idea what the celebration was for. (OK, perhaps not the best example; some parties clearly need no reason.) But as a community builder, it's vital to provide details about what you're trying to accomplish and what kind of help you need.

Hosting revolves around designing an engaging experience that draws out the unique contributions from the group. In the same way that a great party host considers a multitude of details – everything from the flowers on the table to making sure introverts will feel comfortable – facilitating community events is about hosting a welcoming and engaging experience. That often involves connecting participants to one another and then stepping back to let them craft their own experience.

Harvesting is about identifying common themes and patterns and summarizing those for the group. Without a strong closing, a community experience can fizzle out. This may be, at least in part, explained by a concept known as the peak-end rule. Backed by research, this states that people tend to judge an experience based on the most significant peak moment (when you feel the strongest emotions) and it's end, rather than the entirety of the experience. Your memory of an experience is not the average of your overall experience, or even the sum of your experience. Instead, it's defined almost entirely by the peak and end.

As a host, you should consider how to weave in wonder and create memorable experiences for your community, and then close with a strong harvest, as that is what most will remember as they walk away.

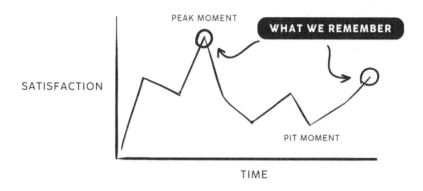

The peak-end rule illustrates what we remember from an event.

At 3 Dots, everyone beamed as we shared what we learned from our design charrettes, their smiles confirming that we had fully heard them. Then it was time to repeat the process all over again.

Using the community commitment curve as a model, we shared a new invitation. This time, we would host a second round of charrettes for people who could specifically assist with various design elements. We had sessions where community members came up with a budget and plan to install our sound system, stage lighting, and gallery hanging system. We had groups meet to explore how to coordinate activities with musicians, artists, and poets. We met with videographers to document the process and spoke with journalists who wrote articles about what was unfolding.

By the end of a three-week sprint, our story was circulating widely around town. We could extend our reach beyond early adopters to the community because we had created a simple and compelling message and found tangible ways to invite people into the story.

Four months later, we officially opened our doors after finishing renovations. We had hundreds of people visit, and we hadn't spent a dime on marketing. We relied entirely on community members being deeply invested in our message and sharing the story with their networks. Once our space was open to the public, we continued to repeat this process and went on to win awards for being the best community space in town.

These techniques work when you find ways to weave the personal experience of people in your community into the collective story of your organization. Our community saw themselves – their ideas, challenges, journey, and friends – in our space.

They had all experienced the challenge of trying to find like-minded creative individuals in town. They had been searching for a space to hang out between work and home where they could feel safe being their authentic selves. By allowing community members to be the hero of the story and serving as their guide, we could support their needs and build a space around that. In turn, they shared their story and how they were able to contribute to this vision with others.

As you work on inviting people into a clear message, remember to frame yourself as the guide and always leave a clear call-to-action for the community to join you. Once you have a clear message developed, you can then start thinking about how you want to get noticed.

CHAPTER 5.2

STAND OUT

WHEN I GOT THE INVITATION, I knew I had to say yes.

I was asked to come to the NASA Jet Propulsion Laboratory in California to join an invite-only event aimed at scaling global social innovations. This was my kind of jam! Nike, NASA, the U.S. Agency for International Development, and the State Department were partnering to host the event and had invited social entrepreneurs from around the world. Without giving it too much thought, I packed my bags and was off.

As I entered JPL, I knew I was in a different world from my small hometown in central Pennsylvania. I found my seat next to a lifesize replica of the Mars Rover, aptly named Curiosity.

I had met a friend on the Educate 20/20 road trip who just happened to be an astronaut (I know, pretty cool, right?), and he had invited me to join. We were working on a project together inspired by the co.space, and he thought this would be a good event for us to connect. I quickly discovered, however, that I might have been out of my league.

Waiting for the event to start, I looked through the program and noticed two groups of people in attendance: industry experts and social innovators. I would have felt far more comfortable in the latter group, yet somehow, I found myself in the industry expert category. I couldn't even tell my mom what industry I was in based on my current career path, so I certainly didn't feel like an expert in a specific field.

Realizing this would be a much longer three days than I thought, I tried to blend in and not draw too much attention to myself. I didn't want to get noticed for the wrong reasons.

As the event kicked off, the organizers explained that the experts would assemble in small groups for the three days we were there, and every 90 minutes, a new social innovator would join our group to share their work. The job of the experts was to share whatever resources we had with the social innovators.

Here's more or less how my first round went. An innovator came to our table working on sustainable textiles. The guy to my left revealed that he oversaw all of the supply chain efforts for Walmart. He offered the innovator access to all of his manufacturers across China. The guy across from me, wearing super snazzy shoes, revealed that he was the head of design for Nike. He offered to run the textiles through his design department to determine if they could be used with their products. The guy to my right wrote a check with more zeros in it than I had ever seen put on one sheet of paper. And what did I have to offer? I told him I could help him work on the color scheme for his logo.

Needless to say, I was in way too deep. I was 26 and suddenly found myself pretending to be an expert on topics I knew nothing about. Every 90 minutes, I was required to reveal to everyone all over again that I had no resources to offer anyone. Despite my best attempts to blend in with the big organizations around me, I couldn't help but feel like I stuck out. At least I wasn't alone. My good friend imposter syndrome joined me for the next three days and was a constant companion.

I did my best to keep it together and act cool. People tell you to "fake it 'til you make it" all the time. But I had a hard time confidently convincing myself that any facade I put on would fool the others.

On the second evening, the organizers hosted a large party at a private house overlooking downtown Hollywood. We sat down to a fancy dinner, where butlers served us our food at tables floating over a pool.

I found myself standing along the railing, admiring the views of the city skyline below, trying not to stand out too much when an older gentleman approached. I asked him how he enjoyed his time, and tried to make small talk for a bit. Then I asked for his name and what he did. He paused, as if I should have known the answer, and proceeded to share that he ran NASA. I froze. I probably should have known that. I was not doing so well at faking it, or keeping a low profile.

But with one day left, I figured there wasn't much more that could go wrong. I just needed to avoid drawing attention to myself.

On that final day, we all gathered at JPL once more to see what the innovators had been able to do with the offered support. People cheered, and prizes were awarded. Then my astronaut friend took the stage.

He explained that as he was retiring soon, he wanted to give one final talk. The folks in this room were some of his closest friends and colleagues; unlike myself, he was used to hanging out in these circles. Instead of his typical presentation, he wanted to use his time to share some projects he was working on with fellow collaborators in the audience that gave him hope for our future.

He didn't tell me this was happening, and it quickly occurred to me that I was working on a project with him. That was the reason I was here after all. He dove right into his slides and started showing the websites of a couple other projects. Not realizing that this was part of the plan, I decided it would be wise to double-check our website.

It had been a little while since I'd visited the site, given that we were still developing the concept. I didn't realize we were at the point where we might start sharing it publicly. But in a few minutes, many really important people would be going to the site, so that ship had sailed.

I pulled my phone into my lap and, as discreetly as possible, typed in the URL. There are certain moments when your heart races so fast that you are afraid folks can audibly hear it beating, those moments in life when you start to panic and honestly have no clue what you will do next. As soon as I hit enter, the URL redirected, and the reverberations of my thumping heart seemed to bounce loudly off the replica of the Curiosity rover.

Somehow, the website changed from a very innocent project about creating social change to one that showed photos that were far too lewd to describe in this book, let alone display at JPL in front of the head of NASA and countless others. Our site had been hacked.

I covered my phone screen as quickly as I could. I was sitting in the front row at a large table of experts, and there were media cameras and leaders from around the world surrounding me. Any one of them might have caught that on their livestream.

Yet that level of embarrassment would pale compared to what might soon happen if my friend presenting on stage were to pull up the URL on the big screen in his final talk as an astronaut before retiring. I was dripping in sweat.

I frantically ran through my options. There was no way I could change things on the backend while sitting in the front row. JPL probably has super fancy technology radars anyway that catch people looking at indecent images on their computers. There was no way to send a secret hand signal to my friend who was presenting to tell him to skip past our slide. And getting up to sprint out the side door seemed a bit dramatic.

I was running out of options. At any moment, I would be publicly humiliated. I'd also most definitely lose my invitation to be an expert the following year, not that that was on my mind at the time. There was only one option left.

Before I left for the event, Christian and I agreed that he would take a break from work for the first time in four years. Christian worked harder than most people I knew, always pursuing a new project or finding a way to sustain our humble nonprofit in those early days. At this very moment, he was lounging on the beach with his girlfriend, and we had both agreed that I would not bug him under any circumstances. So much for our agreement, I calculated, as I sent a desperate text his way: "SOS."

The minute it took for him to respond felt like an eternity. He was blissfully unaware of my panicked state.

"Yes … ??" he responded, knowing that he probably didn't want to hear whatever I was about to share.

I hurriedly explained to him the problem and asked if he had any way to fix it. Christian is one of those guys who enjoys a good prank. So in the silence that proceeded, I knew he was deliberating about whether to bail out his business partner or pretend like he didn't receive my text.

For some reason, his better judgment prevailed, and he agreed to help. Somehow, from the comfort of his beach chair in the sand, he managed to redirect the URL website on the backend. He couldn't figure out how we had been hacked, but he managed to change the URL at least so that it was now redirected to one of our other ventures. It wasn't an ideal solution – but any duct-taped fix was better than the alternative.

Minutes later, my friend highlighted our project on the big screen. He never pulled the website up but shared the link with all of those in the audience. Christian had miraculously saved the day.

The presentation came to a close, and the event started to wrap up. I only needed to skate by for one more hour without being noticed. Then they handed me the microphone.

In the final debrief, the event organizer walked over to me and shared how much they appreciated my perspective that week. Having someone who wasn't tethered to a specific industry, who had a youthful and creative flare to his suggestions, and who wasn't constrained by the way things typically worked was what they valued about my contribution.

Here I was the whole week trying not to get noticed and pretending to blend in with the experts who had decades of experience on me. Yet all along, they were noticing me because I didn't blend in.

———

As Brené Brown points out, "You either walk inside your story and own it, or you stand outside your story and hustle for your worthiness." Sometimes with our community building projects, we try hard to fit the mold of established, professional, and expert groups in our town. When we get to a place where we want to take our project into the community, we try to package ourselves to look like a well-established organization. We contort what makes us unique – the fact that we are grassroots leaders working on emergent, bottom-up ideas – and try to pretend to be something we're not. This can be exhausting and, more often than not, it's counterproductive.

We then begin creating monitoring and evaluation plans, theories of change, staff hierarchies, and spreadsheets to blend in with the experts who have been doing this work far longer than we have. We get overwhelmed by the fact that we don't have multi-person design teams to build professional websites or a PR professional who can craft a press release for us. I'm not arguing against those things; there is a time and a place for them. But consider what unique perspective your project brings to the community. Find ways to get noticed for that, rather than trying to imitate how larger nonprofits or businesses run their operations. Your greatest source of influence in conveying your story is your unique perspective and style.

You probably don't have access to robust supply chains, world-renowned design departments, or excessive amounts of cash.

Rather than trying to articulate your story in the way others who have more experience might, find ways to get noticed for what makes you unique. In what ways can you promote your message to stand out and break the script in your community?

Large organizations get the word out about what they're doing by spending large sums of cash to ratchet up marketing and advertising. It's estimated that the average American encounters anywhere from 5,000 to 10,000 advertisements per day. Considering there are only 1,440 minutes in a day, we are bombarded by marketing nearly 24/7.

Given that you likely don't have a massive advertising budget, you can't rely on paid promotion to reach your community. So as you articulate a compelling story and think about ways to share it with your community, you have to take a different approach. Instead of relying on financial capital to amplify your message, you have to use your social capital and a healthy dose of creative imagination. "Guerrilla marketers do not rely on the brute force of an outsized marketing budget," business writer Jay Conrad Levinson notes in his book "Guerilla Marketing." "Instead, they rely on the brute force of a vivid imagination."

Having a distinct way to distinguish your message from the crowd is critical for gaining support. As Trailhead was launching (before it would eventually morph into 3 Dots), we knew our message was focused on connecting and funding creative individuals. But our target audience wasn't connected to the creative spaces around town at that time. We had to find ways to spread the word in places where our people might already hang out – everywhere from coffee shops to grocery stores and hiking trails to libraries. So I bought another recumbent bike.

DESIGNING CREATIVE COMMUNITIES

But this time, I didn't cover it with a blue chameleon. I had learned that lesson. The chameleon taught me the importance of framing a clear and inviting message. I also learned how to creatively place my message in front of people in unsuspecting yet impactful ways.

For nearly a year, I searched on craigslist for a used recumbent bike called an ELF (which stands for Electric, Light, Fun). Eventually, I found an older couple selling one in North Carolina, over 500 miles from where I lived. But the price was right, so I hitched up a U-Haul trailer and drove down to pick it up.

The vehicle looks like a giant orange egg with a solar panel on top, pedals to power it forward, and two seats inside front to back. As soon as I got it back to State College, I plastered the outside with massive stickers that said, "We connect and fund your ideas to make Centre County an awesome place to call home." I then glued plastic waterproof containers to either side and put flyers in them that said, "We want to give you $1,000."

No one in my community had ever seen a contraption like this, and for the next few years, while building Trailhead, I used it as my primary vehicle to get around town. I frequently took my dog with me as we cruised down the bike paths to work, both of us with our tongues flapping in the wind. I usually wore a pirate jacket because something just feels right about wearing a pirate jacket while biking in a bright orange egg.

It's impossible not to stare at an ELF (which is why my wife prefers not to ride in it). Everywhere I went, people approached me. They were curious about the bike, but the conversation always led to asking about what Trailhead was and if we really did give out no-strings-attached grants every month. We were an organization designed to support creative innovations, and the ELF was simply a tangible example of what that could look like. Our message matched the means of delivery.

When I went out to dinner, I would watch from the window as people peaked inside the bike, wondering where the owner was. They'd curiously take handfuls of flyers that directed them to our website. Business owners would often come outside and ask to take a photo with the bike beside their sign to post on their social media accounts.

I took that bike everywhere. I drove it deep into the woods for hikes with my dog. (Riding through the woods in a bright orange egg ensures you're not missed during hunting season in Pennsylvania.) When I wasn't downtown, I took it on long rides in the countryside. And everywhere I went, people approached me wanting to learn more about Trailhead. I never had to force the conversation because their curiosity had already been piqued.

Curiosity is a powerful storytelling tool that can elevate smaller, grassroots efforts above the noise of mainstream marketing. Studies have found that 48 hours after hearing a message, we only remember 25% of what we heard. But curiosity has been shown to play an essential role in increasing memory and retention.

In one study published in the journal Cell Press, researchers found that curiosity not only helps you remember the thing you are curious about, but also other unrelated information. As the lead researcher, Matthias Gruber of the University of California at Davis notes, "Curiosity may put the brain in a state that allows it to learn and retain any kind of information, like a vortex that sucks in what you are motivated to learn, and also everything around it." The same study showed that when people's curiosity is piqued, their brain activity increases in the regions that form new memories, as well as those that transmit dopamine signals. In this way, curiosity activates the same parts of our brain that cause us to crave chocolate or nicotine.

Imagine if the Mars rover, Curiosity, were parked in the middle of your downtown. People would naturally approach and want to learn more. That's the power of a good story.

There are lots of creative ways you can harness curiosity. In the UK, a team of designers and community leaders decided to bring the inanimate objects around their city to life. They launched a project called "Hello Lamp Post," which lets community members have conversations with everyday items, such as fire hydrants, benches, and cranes. Signs are posted near the object telling people to text, for example, "Tree #3" at a certain number, and then they are suddenly engaged in a text conversation with that object.

Tree #3: "Good afternoon, we haven't met before. Can I ask, what brings you to this part of town?"

Person: "I'm going home; you just happen to live on my route."

Tree #3: "Oh right! The last person I spoke to said: 'I was taking a shortcut on my way to work, then I got distracted and started talking to a tree.'"

The project is designed to engage citizens in local decision-making and strengthen their sense of belonging to the area. In this example, the team has found a powerful way of incorporating playful placemaking that they developed through early prototypes into their eventual story and project.

———

Community builders can also find ways to position their careers in ways that uniquely stand out for all the right reasons. A few years ago, I traveled through Helena, Arkansas, a tiny town of 10,000 people along the Mississippi River. I was there to meet with the founders of Thrive, a community-powered design group.

The organization was launched by two designers, Will Staley and Terrance Clark, who had been living in Brooklyn and graduated from one of the world's top design schools. New York is full of creative marketing agencies with well-established reputations. But their dream was to create a social impact design firm in Helena. Rather than replicate what bigger organizations were doing, they decided to flip the approach. Thanks to a lower cost of living, they could continue offering design services to big clients, but only needed a fraction of the work to cover their bills. Rather than try and blend in with the countless other design agencies in big cities, they positioned themselves to uniquely stand out by setting up shop in a small town.

With the remaining hours in their day, they committed to launching a community center. That's Thrive: half design agency, half community center. Will, Terrance, and their team ran entrepreneurial bootcamp programs by creating the Helena Entrepreneur Center. They organized a monthly street festival and art walk called the Cherry Street Fair, which provides a marketplace for local artists and merchants. They inspired a renewed pride in their downtown. Over time, they built design residencies and internship programs in partnership with local schools. They developed programs, which provided vital mentorship, that allowed them to create thriving makerspaces and design studios that students can use. This gives young people a way to develop their creative talents locally without having to leave town.

From the beginning, they were committed to a simple mission: Empower communities to thrive with thoughtful design to minimize brain drain in the region. By focusing on the parts of their story that made them unique, the designers stood out and got noticed.

Clients began working with them on design projects, which generated revenue for the organization, because they knew the profits would be invested in youth mentorship and creative placemaking programs. As a result, the Thrive team has begun to recruit more people to move to Helena and help transform the area. As they share on their website:

"It's easy to write Helena off as a place that will never again live up to its former glory. But we at Thrive, along with so many others who call Helena home, wholeheartedly believe in the tremendous potential for good things to happen here."

Articulating your story in a way that stands out helps you focus on what makes your project unique. As you lean into what makes your project different within the community, others will start to notice and join you.

A blue chameleon car will get you noticed, but it won't tell a clear story. A solar-powered bike inviting people to submit similarly innovative ideas for a grant will get you noticed while also sending a clear message. Curiosity, when harnessed properly, will help your message stand out from the crowd while also being memorable. As entrepreneur and author Seth Godin writes, "You can either fit in or stand out. Not both."

Once you determine how you want to get noticed, you can begin thinking about the best ways to leverage the media landscape to elevate your message and project.

NAVIGATE THE MEDIA LANDSCAPE

ONCE YOU HAVE A CLEAR message and plan for how you want to get noticed, you can focus on packaging your message so that it will get shared widely. This requires some media savvy. Learning how to work hand-in-hand with media partners is crucial to reach your community and increase participation.

There are four key components to consider when working with the media. First, you need to develop a digital destination for your work, which might include a brand, website, or blog. Then you can leverage your relationships with local journalists, tap into your social networks, and identify ways to garner external validation. That could include connecting to case studies, podcasts, or competitions. Collectively, these media components will help creatively raise the profile of your story.

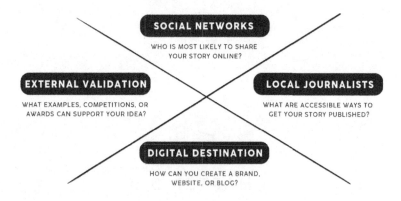

Four elements to consider when navigating the media.

First and foremost, if you want to leverage media exposure to get more people involved in your work, you need to have somewhere to send them. It's not enough to have a story written about your project if there's no clear way for people to follow up and get involved. So you need to make your project look official.

One of my favorite organizations is the U.S. Department of Arts and Culture. With cultural agents spread out all around the country, the USDAC exists to inspire creativity and social imagination toward shaping a culture of empathy, equity, and belonging.

They host a wide range of programs. For their annual People's State of the Union, poets and artists nationwide share their vision for the country's future. USDAC Citizen Artist Salons convene community builders via video-based gatherings to discuss and share resources on creative placemaking. They produce guides on everything from hosting arts-based community dialogues to starting your own Super PAC, which in this case is a Participatory Arts Coalition.

Everything is decentralized and people-powered. Their members shape how the department focuses its energy and resources. They regularly enlist new members to start USDAC Outposts in new cities with minimal red tape.

By this point, you are likely wondering, "How have I never heard of this department before?" Think of all of the other government agencies you are familiar with; why is it that the USDAC hasn't made it on your radar? Well, it's not because they are bad at navigating the media landscape. It's because they have no affiliation with the U.S. government.

The USDAC is not a federal agency but a grassroots network created by everyday community builders. The inspiration came when one of the founders, Adam Horowitz, lived in Colombia as a Fulbright Scholar and worked with the country's Ministry of Culture. He wondered how it was possible that the United States didn't have a group dedicated to culture in the same way Colombia did. Frustrated at the lack of such a group, he created the USDAC.

Community builders love taking initiative, and they rarely wait for permission. Adam designed yard signs and eventually a logo that looks just like a government seal. He had a simple website built, and began recruiting members.

As soon as the idea was formalized with a logo and website, people got behind it. Before Adam knew it, the concept spread, and the USDAC was operating in all 50 states (just like a genuine federal entity might). Relying on a healthy dose of collective social imagination, the USDAC became a thriving community.

Although I've never tried to create my own federal agency, I've found that packaging your idea into something official-looking is an important step in articulating your story.

Nowadays, anyone can build a simple website, or at the very least create a Facebook page or publish a blog post. Having a digital home base that you can direct people to from a story or your own marketing materials helps legitimize the work you're doing in the eyes of your community. It also provides a starting point for people to get involved. Add a simple logo – even if you have to get it designed by your neighbor's nephew – and that idea you first developed with a few friends and followers has suddenly evolved into a proper project.

Now that you have a digital home for your message, it's time to insert it into the media landscape. Each town is different, but regardless of what that looks like where you live, your goal is to discover how to get your story covered. You need to find the entry point.

I'm not an expert in the changing landscape of media and journalism, but if there's one thing I've learned, it's that it's not too difficult to get media coverage. When thinking about leveraging local news, begin by identifying where the most accessible starting point is to get a story placed into the media landscape.

In a university town like State College, we have many young journalists – students who are writing for their college newspaper or completing an assignment for a class. Student journalists have always been the entrance to the media landscape for me.

Journalists – especially students – need great stories. As a community builder, you are surrounded by great stories.

I was in a newsroom at a local paper when a high-pitched buzzer went off over the PA system, followed by a police dispatch.

The editor explained that the buzzer was connected to the local police department, and every time an incident report came in, the journalists received an announcement. The buzzer was jarring, and I couldn't imagine how anyone could get work done with that sitting above their desk.

Imagine yourself as the antidote to that annoying buzzer. You are the person bringing positive stories of change and possibility to journalists who are otherwise surrounded by the high-pitched buzzers (literal or figurative) announcing negative police reports.

The most effective approach to position yourself this way is to keep in regular communication with journalists, and share simple stories with them. The more clearly you can articulate the story of your project and why it matters to their readers, the more likely they are to cover it and share the story with their followers on social media.

Staff journalists used to write all of their own articles and tended to do more of their own reporting. But that's shifting. With the rise of the internet, social media, and blogging, many of the articles you read online are submitted by freelance writers or based on press releases written by PR agencies. This worries me in the sense that almost anything can be pushed and perceived as newsworthy. And certainly, some publications still thrive on original reporting and hold a higher standard than others. But in the same breath, you can use this new norm as a way to amplify your story and garner coverage.

This is where student journalists have been critical for me. Nearly every bit of media coverage I've received for a project, venture, or initiative I've led started with a story written by a student journalist. It's not always the most well-written, but it gets the conversation going. Our local newspaper pays attention to what's published in the student newspaper and frequently covers similar stories. That can lead to coverage by monthly magazines, our university press, and the occasional NPR interview.

Over the years, I've been able to build friendships with local journalists and storytellers, which means I now don't need to always start at the bottom of the media food chain. But my approach remains the same. I make sure to regularly check in with my media friends, see how I can provide value to their world, and if they are looking for any stories – especially human-interest stories – share a few.

As I frame my pitches to journalists, I always keep the following three questions in mind: Why now? Why is this news? Who cares? By framing my work in a way that aligns with the journalist's needs, I'm more likely to have it covered. As Maya Angelou writes,

"If you want what you're saying heard, then take your time and say it so that the listener will actually hear it."

The State of Journalism 2020 report published by Muck Rack found that "93% of journalists prefer to be pitched via email" and that 85% of journalists said that "email remains the best way to maintain a professional relationship," followed by Twitter or in-person.

I make sure to pass on stories about other projects in town as well so as to not be self-serving. The goal is to build a relationship of trust and discovery so that they know they can always check in to discover what sort of innovative things are happening in the local community.

The other form of media to leverage is social media and word of mouth promotion. This has been critical to every venture I've run. I'm not interested in my neighbor's latest picture of her dinner or my high school friend posting photos of her cat (although I will admit, I occasionally post pictures of my own cat). Instead, I've always seen social media as my source for discovering the pulse of my community. I'm interested to know:

- What projects are people pursuing?
- What new connections are being made?
- What resources are being shared?
- What frustrations are people venting about online?

Based on what I find, I can respond with creative new projects that offer a solution. When someone complains about a bland skyscraper being built downtown, I find ways to connect those developers with muralists. And I often rely on private Facebook groups to uncover new resources and opportunities that would be much harder for me to find through traditional email Listservs or newsgroups.

Social media also allows me to personalize my messages. There's a big difference between receiving an email, phone call, Facebook message, or personal text. I don't have everyone's phone number, but I can easily find people on social media. I regularly Facebook message the leaders of my local government and downtown businesses to get the inside scoop on what's going on, and I am often scanning my list of friends to remind myself of people I haven't checked in with for a while to see how they're doing.

In keeping in touch with my network, when I have media stories to share about my work, I can ask a wide range of contacts if they can promote it with their friends as well. As it turns out, garnering news coverage is half the battle; figuring out how to get the story widely shared throughout your community is just as important.

In a 2017 study, researchers from the University of Chicago teamed up with the American Press Institute to explore the role that trust plays online when news articles are shared on social media. In their study, they had participants review a news article titled "Don't let the scale fool you: Why you could still be at risk for diabetes." In some instances, the story was attributed to a reputable news source, the AP, and other times to a fictional news source they called the "Daily News Review." They had the subjects rank the articles based on a few criteria, such as how factual or entertaining the articles were.

But there was one more important variable the researchers measured: who shared the article with the participants. Sometimes it came from someone they trusted, like Oprah or the surgeon general, and other times from someone who they previously indicated they did not trust.

Researchers found that "people who see an article from a trusted sharer, but one written by an unknown media source, have much more trust in the information than people who see the same article from a reputable media source shared by a person they do not trust." The takeaway was profound: The trust in the messenger has more weight than the trust in the news source.

We've all seen how this has negatively played out on social

media with the rise of fake news and extreme polarization. But the positive spin from studies like this is that when building grassroots efforts, you can lean on the trust of your messengers – your early adopters – to recruit others. People are more likely to feel confident in supporting efforts that are broadcast or validated by friends they trust. And it's not nearly as important that you're covered by the most well-established newsgroup in town; you simply need to have your story told by a media outlet.

Media coverage is helpful to establish your credibility. But there's another component that's just as important. You need to find external groups, or experts outside your community, that support or validate your idea.

This could be as simple as finding related case studies and leaders in other communities doing similar work. You can point to these external groups and examples to justify your idea. Or you can work with outside groups who can validate what you're doing.

To turn the co.space idea into a credible organization in our town, we had to establish legitimacy. We built websites and encouraged local news to cover the story, but ultimately knew we had to find external groups that could strengthen our idea's validity.

When I was traveling through Europe after participating in the Oasis game, I stumbled across someone who worked for a relatively obscure nonprofit. We stayed in touch; and when I started posting about our new venture on social media, she reached out.

They were creating an awards program called the Green Economy Eco-Business Innovation Initiative, or GEEBIZ. It was a mouthful, and not a single person in the entire state of Pennsylvania had heard of the group. Nonetheless, we were selected as one of the winners. We used that recognition to leapfrog into another online competition – this one simply requiring lots of your friends to vote for you to decide the winner. There was no judging on the merit of the idea or the possibility of it becoming an actual project. It was simply a popularity and persistence contest. But by this point, we had built relationships with people across the community. Over two weeks, we repeatedly asked for their support, and we ultimately won the online competition.

That raised our profile and an article was published on a national news site covering what we were doing. We hadn't even purchased the home yet, but the story resonated with external groups in a way we never expected. Soon after, we received an email from our friend, the astronaut, who would go on to be a collaborator with us for the coming year or two, as well as a message from MTV. They were interested in filming a reality TV series on the co.space.

We never ended up partnering with MTV, which offered to fund nearly the entire project with product placements. ("This tenant is getting a great start to his morning thanks to the help of his Gillette razor!") The risk of letting our story get shaped by an outside influence was too much in the early days of our project. We feared we would lose control.

But while we never formalized a partnership with the iconic entertainment brand, we still leveraged that external credibility when talking with local groups. Students were fascinated by the idea of living somewhere that was TV-worthy. Our local government paid more attention to our pitch when they knew it had the chance to influence their town's public image.

As hard as you try, it can be challenging to get the validation you need from locally established groups. I work in lots of small towns, and they are great at shutting down new ideas thanks to old guard systems that support the status quo. That's why when external groups take notice of your work, it's so important to leverage that opportunity.

Short of receiving unsolicited emails from MTV or NASA, there are lots of other ways you can leverage external groups to build your credibility too. Fellowships, podcasts, speaking gigs, crowdfunding campaigns, and testimonials are all great ways to strengthen your idea.

The reality is that not every idea will take flight. But when you're able to connect with the right people and seize timely opportunities, you can significantly increase your chances of success. Consider how you can leverage your strengths to get connected and raise the profile of your idea in your community. It's not enough to expect people to stumble across your work; you must actively put it on their radar.

Trying to win online competitions may not be your preferred form of external validation. Still, I would challenge you to find at least one way to generate buzz outside your town that can be leveraged to increase interest in your town. Your goal is not to get distracted by racking up awards or recognition. Instead, you want to determine how you can use outside recognition to open doors locally and draw more attention to your work.

That's your goal when articulating your story. Create a clear narrative which is easy to share and will resonate with your target audience. Determine what unique part of your project you want to highlight so that it stands out, and start making that a centerpiece of your messaging.

Build a website, leverage local media coverage, and seek out external groups and similar examples that can bolster your idea's credibility. As you do this, others in your community will feel compelled to get behind the unfolding narrative of your work. By that point, partners are often curious to find out how they, too, can get involved.

STEP 6

SUSTAIN EFFORTS WITH PARTNERS

YOU MAY HAVE SEEN PUBLIC pianos in towns around the country. It's a simple concept: Place a few pianos outside in public spaces and invite strangers to gather and play. It's a perfect example of creative placemaking.

Many communities are doing this now, mainly because there's ample research showing it works to bring people together in public places. You don't have to look hard to find external validation for the idea. But when we were first getting started at New Leaf, public pianos were surprisingly bold and divisive for our community.

During those early days at New Leaf, while endlessly searching craigslist, we began to notice that lots of people were trying to sell – or simply give away – pianos. Never ones to turn away free resources, we reached out to many who posted that they were giving away pianos. We told them we'd use the pianos to raise funds for other nonprofits through a public art project.

Soon, we had four pianos, and each had a mural representing a different local nonprofit painted on it. One was dedicated to environmental justice, another focused on international development, and the others promoted volunteering and cross-cultural dialogue.

Our town's arts festival was approaching, so on the morning of the event, we wheeled the pianos out on the sidewalk. We chained them to any bench or tree we could find and watched as people began to play.

It didn't take long before folks started making connections, just as we'd intended. Older ladies were teaching young middle school students a song. Busy families took a break from their day as their youngest jumped up to play. Many of our partners were thrilled to see our vision come to fruition, from the mayor to our local arts festival organizers.

We went back to our office to get some work done. After all, pianos alone weren't paying the bills. Then around lunch, we went back out to check on them. I skipped across the street, excited to see one of our first public art projects put to good use.

But as I came to the spot where I was pretty sure we'd left one piano hours earlier, I found only an empty sidewalk. I ran to another street corner, where I was sure we had placed a second piano. But that sidewalk, too, was empty.

Every piano was missing, along with the chains we'd used to secure them. I was either the victim of a bizarre piano heist or an elaborate prank pulled off by my friends. At least those were the only two scenarios I could conceive of at that moment.

A little while later, we got a phone call. That's when I learned that while we had lots of partners who supported us, we didn't have the right partners.

I'd never heard of the public works department before. "Parks and Recreation" wasn't popular on TV yet, so I had no clue what they did or why we should have partnered with the department. It would have been nice to have learned through a simple conversation that when you want to put pianos in public places, it's a good idea to coordinate this with public works. Instead, I found this out after they'd dumped our pianos in a pile of broken wood and ivory on my business partner's driveway.

As the truck unloaded the pianos, they told us they were removed from the streets because they "posed a danger to our community." I had a hard time imagining how young kids or elderly ladies playing sweet classical tunes might be dangerous.

They clarified by saying that we had created multiple fire hazards by placing large wooden objects on the sidewalk. Public works was worried people might light them on fire. It seemed like a bit of a stretch to me, but you never know with college students (or devious grandparents).

The next day, the story of the failed pianos found its way into the newspaper. In the article's comments section online, readers listed all of the other wooden things one finds downtown that no one had ever considered lighting on fire before. It turned out that the rest of the community thought the decision by public works to remove the pianos was just as ridiculous as we did.

But because of those pianos, we learned a lot about being strategic in developing partnerships. Equally as important, we learned that pianos aren't as forgiving as ball pit balls. When you handle pianos roughly, they don't revert back to their former shape. We found ourselves staring at a pile of broken pianos that no longer provided much value to society, other than as good kindling for bonfires.

For the next year, we regularly reminded ourselves of the importance of assembling the right partners as we toasted marshmallows in our backyard over the splintered remains of our creative placemaking project. It takes a long time to burn a pile of pianos.

———————

Nearly a decade later, the community seems to have warmed up to the idea of putting innocent instruments around town. Progress tends to take time. Frequently you fail, and hopefully learn from what didn't work before you succeed.

When 3 Dots opened, we put a painted piano on our sidewalk. This time around, the piano remained in place, and it was the talk of the town. It was featured in news articles as one of the best places to take a photo. It was also widely known on social media as a place people gathered late at night to sing with strangers. People may not have known what happened inside our doors, but they most definitely knew about our purple piano.

That one piano reflected so much of the progress I'd witnessed in our town over the previous decade. More than simply being a conversation piece, it represented so much of what I had learned about community building in State College.

Public pianos reinforced the importance of showing, not just telling, our community what was possible. This is key when you start working with partners, who naturally will want to see what you've done rather than just hearing about your successes in a pitch. And my public piano odyssey taught me some invaluable lessons about unexpected ways that partnerships can emerge.

Although I had started an arts space and was responsible for putting musical instruments on our streets, I actually knew very little about music. Epic air guitar solos aside, I don't play any instruments.

Six months after opening 3 Dots, someone came into our space and asked me how our piano was in such good shape and so well-tuned. I told them we must have gotten a really nice piano donated off craigslist. I didn't realize that these things actually need to be tuned and aren't designed to sit outside.

The visitor assured me that there was no way our piano could sound that good without someone regularly tuning it. I assured him no one on our team had touched it. He left convinced I didn't know what I was talking about, and I spent the rest of the day Googling information on the importance of tuning a piano.

Instruments don't sound their best without this type of maintenance. Yet, somehow, our piano seemed to magically remain in tune. How could this be? No one on my team could figure it out.

A few months passed. Then one day while I was working, I happened to glance out the window and saw someone playing who clearly knew what he was doing. It was captivating. His music filled the streets. Cars remained idle at the adjacent intersection. Drivers were so mesmerized by his tunes they forgot to step on the gas when the light turned green. I went outside to introduce myself and thank him for stopping by to play. He continued jamming out, oblivious to the wonderful commotion all around him that he was creating.

Then, as he finished, he lifted the piano's lid and started messing around with the wires beneath. I felt the urge to ask him to stop, but he was so confident that I just let him continue.

He got a little spray bottle out of his backpack, sprayed it on some keys, and wiggled a few more wires. He put the piano lid back down, and without saying much, started to walk off. I had to jog to catch up, and asked him what he had been doing. That's when I discovered that he had been tuning the piano for the last nine months.

Without anyone asking, he had seen the piano sitting outside one day and thought he would check to make sure it sounded good. The first time he made a minor adjustment here and there. But a few weeks later, he returned with his tools and did a proper tuning. He had been quietly visiting our street corner ever since to tune our piano. He never introduced himself or asked for permission. He saw a need and he addressed it.

When designing participatory community initiatives, you can create a culture that invites others to lend their skills without even needing to ask people to do this. Partnership building can sometimes feel frustrating, especially in towns that are not receptive to innovative new ideas. But when you're patient and persistent in following through with your idea, you'll frequently find partners emerge when you least expect them and offer their skills to meet your unique needs.

I never asked our volunteer piano tuner how often he came by. I don't know his qualifications, and to this day, I don't have his name or contact information. But I trust that our piano will be just fine. The best partnerships are always built on trust. Our space was built on the belief that needs will get filled by those most capable and motivated. If you invite the community's active participation, people will seek out a partnership.

If our friend happens to leave or move to another town, I'm sure another mystery piano tuner will emerge. When your community sees their town as a canvas, they find any opportunity they can to make their mark on it.

To get to this point, the last step of the CANVAS framework is to focus on sustaining your work through partnerships.

Over the years, I've learned what's required in this phase. You must:

1. Seek transformation, not transactions.

2. Stop pitching, start serving.

3. Rely on the collective trust of others.

CHAPTER 6.1

SEEK TRANSFORMATION, NOT TRANSACTIONS

YOU MAY HAVE NOTICED A theme by this point in the book. Community building is all about relationships. Establishing those relationships requires building trust, having empathy, and becoming acquainted with others' authentic stories. In the same way, all successful partnerships are built on trust.

Over the last decade, I have made it a routine to regularly walk the streets of my downtown every few weeks. I drop in on various businesses and community spaces, having no set meeting or purpose other than to hear about what's going on. I've discovered that bringing a dog with you is cheating because everyone opens up when they have the chance to pet a dog for a few minutes.

(If you are stuck finding partners for your project, I recommend rescuing a dog. Or you could start a pet-sitting side business.)

I frequently drop by our local chamber of commerce, the downtown improvement office, and police department. I hang out longer than I should, getting to know tellers at the bank and bike mechanics at the repair shops.

Many organizations and the people who work there are focused on their specific operations and don't have the time to play the role of connector. But as a community builder, I've found it's critical to find ways to carve out time in my schedule to build up social capital in town. You have to invest in relationships long before seeking partners. Connections, and the trust they are built upon, are the currency of community building.

A 2015 report by McKinsey & Company found that the top two reasons partnerships fail are due to a lack of trust and misalignment on the shared objective between partners. If you can focus on getting these two elements right, you're far more likely to be successful. Partnership building is all about alignment and trust.

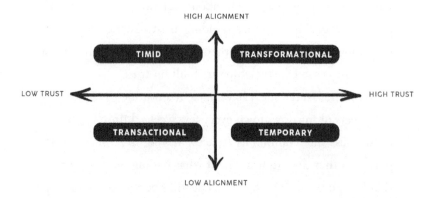

Different types of relationships that can be developed with partners.

Partnerships tend to fall into one of four categories. Partnerships that lack trust or alignment are no more than transactional relationships. Imagine if you approached a business owner you didn't have a relationship with to sponsor a project. If that business doesn't care deeply about your cause, you might be lucky to get a donation or in-kind contribution. And that support would be nothing more than a simple transaction.

Now imagine you have a strong relationship with the business owner you're approaching. Even if your work doesn't perfectly align with their interests, there's a higher likelihood they'll at least provide temporary support. But if it doesn't align with their goals, it's unlikely they will support you in an ongoing capacity. They want to see you succeed, but they won't be as invested in collaborating long-term alongside you.

On the other end of the spectrum, you might find partners who share your vision and want to collaborate, but with whom you haven't yet been able to build trust. These partners are often timid about entering into collaborative relationships. To move these potential partners into the fourth quadrant I outline, you have to invest the time it takes to strengthen the relationship and gain their confidence. This may require leaning into intermediaries in your network.

When partners align with your vision and you've built a high degree of trust, this often leads to impactful transformations. These are the types of partnerships where everyone involved joyfully works hand-in-hand to see the vision sustained in the community.

Yet as hard as you'll try, some partnerships will never materialize. This is not necessarily because you can't find alignment or build trust. Sometimes the timing isn't right.

Prior to running Trailhead, I worked with Christian and Jared (my initial first followers) to start an Escape Room: a room full of clues and puzzles that teams have to solve in order to escape in a set amount of time. We loved the idea of building our own puzzles and designing experiences that help retain young professionals, but we also wanted the business to double as a community center.

Most Escape Rooms have pretty standard themes – everything from pyramids to magicians – but ours would be different. We wanted to highlight the unique parts of our town. Each themed room would reveal stories and facts about State College and help people discover the untapped gems and local organizations they could support.

For example, one room was designed to look like a bike mechanic's shop. During the challenge, teams would learn about different mountain biking trails in the area, how to get a bike permit and what makes State College one of the most bikeable cities in the country. We wanted to fuse together entertainment, education, and community engagement.

Despite our best efforts to launch the company, we couldn't secure the partners we needed. We approached lots of funders who we had previous experience with and who shared our desire to reduce brain drain and create unique social offerings for our town beyond another bar. But the timing never aligned. Escape Happy Valley never became a reality.

But the relationships, trust, and conversations around what was needed for our town grew beyond our project. Over time, new ideas emerged and those same initial conversations with partners led to the creation of Trailhead, and then eventually 3 Dots.

Transformational partnerships are like a team working together to complete an Escape Room puzzle; you have to lean on one another's strengths and have a shared objective. They take time to nurture and with each new clue, you lean more and more on one another to tackle the next challenge. On the other hand, a transactional partnership would be like someone simply telling you the code and walking away. You might be able to get out of that immediate Escape Room, but your team won't have the collective excitement or experience to take on the next challenge together.

As we began renovating 3 Dots, I focused on building partnerships to help us find cheap renovation materials. We had a scrappy budget, and I knew if we were going to be successful, we would need lots of free or inexpensive items. I reminded myself of what was possible through the Oasis game and set out to find partners willing to contribute.

Our need was simple: We had to furnish 3,000 square feet. Specifically, I was looking for funky, bright, unique furniture that would transform our otherwise white-walled space into something that felt alive and dynamic.

For weeks, I regularly visited as many furniture stores as I could, from high-end local boutiques to brand-name big box stores. Most days, I ended up with nothing. Even when things were on sale, we couldn't afford them. At one store, in particular, I became a regular. I would walk in, make my habitual loop around the floor to see if anything was discounted, and then stroll back out to my car where my dog was patiently waiting with the windows rolled down.

One day, the store's manager stopped me. She told me she had noticed that I had been in multiple times and wondered if I needed help or was just looking for a place to sleep during the day. Had I still been sleeping on couches, I may have taken her up on that offer.

I told her what I had shared with many of her employees: that I was starting an arts and innovation space downtown, and our goal was to elevate everything great about our local area. We wanted to showcase what made State College special by designing a welcoming and caring space for those who stepped inside.

That struck a chord.

I could tell something changed in her tone after I mentioned "welcoming and caring." I proceeded to tell her I was looking to build fake indoor trees for the space and needed some funky modern couches.

Up to that point, we'd gotten our furniture exclusively from craigslist. I explained that every night I would reach out to at least a dozen people online and tell them that although I had no money, I would be able to offer them an in-kind tax-deductible donation slip if they wanted to donate their furniture. It worked for the public pianos. Why not try it again?

Surprisingly, at least 20% of the people I reached out to were willing to donate. I had collected all kinds of things, from Apple TVs to red leather couches to funky bedside stands. I planned to continue that approach, but at some point, our space would start to feel like an indoor flea market instead of a trendy arts space.

Her curiosity piqued, the manager told me to follow her upstairs. We went into the kids' playroom, where parents can drop their kids off while looking at furniture. I thought she was going to tell me I could have their ball pit balls. (I already knew how I would fit them in my car.) But instead, she was taking me somewhere private to talk.

As we sat beside the giant rainbow slide, the conversation shifted from my needs to hers. I learned that the furniture store had recently been sold to a group outside of town. A local family had owned the store for many years. Despite being a large furniture provider, the family did things like a small town shop would. They wrote up every invoice and inventory list by hand and focused on old-school relationship-building with their clients. But that was all about to change.

The new owners, she explained, were located out of state and wanted to streamline the entire business. No more paper pads; everything was moving digital. They were restructuring how the managers and employees interacted. Instead of staff having the flexibility and autonomy they'd been accustomed to with the previous ownership, they were now going to have to work within a more rigid corporate hierarchy.

The manager teared up as she spoke at length about the ownership change. I briefly glanced down at my watch and realized we had been in the kids' playroom for nearly an hour. I felt so bad for the employees because they were clearly going through a traumatic transition. But I told her I had a dog in the car and probably had to go soon.

Ignoring my attempt to bow out gracefully, she told me we had more to discuss and that I should bring my dog into the store. I'm sure that was definitely against their new owners' corporate policy, but this seemed like a conversation worth continuing.

I brought my dog in with me, hoping that he wouldn't have the sudden urge to pee on any of their fake trees, and the manager greeted me at the entrance. She told me that in two days, the entire company would be transitioning over to the new digital system. It was the moment their team was all dreading.

Then she offered me an opportunity to partner with her.

Her need was simple: She had lots of furniture that she wouldn't be able to sell, which she wanted to donate. Frustrated with how the new owners were restricting their ability to support local organizations, she wanted to provide her employees with an opportunity to give back to their community before management changed. And she understood that my need was furniture.

So she proposed a partnership. Tomorrow night, I was to return to their store at the last hour of the day before they would switch over to the new system. I was to bring as many trucks as I could. The previous owners allowed them to make occasional in-kind donations, in moderation, to community groups and nonprofits in town. A painting or side table they couldn't sell was always better off in the hands of a local nonprofit.

But in the final hour before the ownership change, the manager granted us a free shopping spree. The new company was doing away with knick-knacks – things like fake trees, wall hangings, rugs, and weird globes. She introduced me to one of her sales reps and told me to walk around the store and take whatever knick-knacks we wanted.

The following day I returned with my business partner, and we loaded car after car with all kinds of things. We picked up fake trees that cost $1,500 apiece. (Who pays that much for an artificial tree? Fortunately, my dog never peed on them.) We carefully arranged funky modern statues into our trunks, precisely the type of thing you would use to turn an empty space into a thriving arts and innovation center. The employee tasked with noting everything we picked tirelessly hand wrote each item down on her pad of paper, jotting "~$1" beside each piece. At the end of the day, we walked out with car loads of items that easily added up to nearly half of our renovation budget.

Had I walked into the furniture store with a fancy sponsorship deck and made a pitch to their manager, we may have gotten a piece or two donated, but it would have felt like nothing more than a transaction. By investing the energy to empathize with and hear the story of where our partner was coming from, we built a relationship and identified how our visions for the future aligned. She may not have wanted to build an arts and innovation space, but the vision my team was creating aligned with her desire to be part of a company that meaningfully contributes to the surrounding community. Empathy leads to partnership building. That's when the most impactful collaborations emerge.

One of my favorite examples of a community that built a transformational space together through partnerships is Urbana-Champaign. In 2000, a group of artists, activists, and community leaders started to meet in their living rooms to explore what it would take to launch a creative space together. They called themselves the Urbana-Champaign Independent Media Center. They envisioned a space where the community could design their own solutions to local challenges while having access to arts and media production resources. They wanted to amplify underrepresented voices and connect social justice leaders, grassroots organizers, technology enthusiasts, and independent artists.

While they searched for space, they approached hundreds of community members and leaders – much as we did when we launched 3 Dots – by asking them if they would be willing to financially contribute to acquiring a space together. Their early adopters quickly started to join, each giving a small amount of money as their story was shared widely around town. After a few years, they had raised $75,000 in donations from early adopters to purchase a building sight unseen.

Eventually, they found a 30,000-square-foot property that housed the U.S. Post Office and was owned by the federal government. Partnership discussions began as they built trust and sought to identify how their needs aligned. They discovered that the Post Office was looking for ways to lower their rent and mortgage payments.

Together, they agreed on a deal where the UCIMC would buy the U.S. Postal Service property for a little over $200,000 in exchange for letting the Post Office stay in the building rent-free for the next 10 years. This satisfied the needs of each partner. UCIMC was able to acquire a large space central to their downtown, and the post office was able to eliminate their rent payment for the next 10 years.

The post office now provides a consistent revenue source as one of the anchor tenants for the space. Today, the building is home to radio stations, makerspaces, independent newspapers, artist studios, and community gathering spaces. They have sponsored more than 40 organizations that have evolved out of the space.

––––––

"The only way to grow trust is to take the time needed to understand differences and find commonalities," notes Dawn Newman, who works on leadership and civic engagement issues with tribal communities, in an article on the University of Minnesota Extension's website. "It seems counter-intuitive to take that time when things need to get done – and things always need to get done. In the long run though, that time can make community networks tighter and more productive."

Partnerships are relationships. And relationships require you to invest the energy to learn more about someone else and discover the needs they have. Nearly every formal partnership I've formed over the last 10 years has emerged from very personal shared moments, the kind where someone may vulnerably open up about themselves in a ball pit. Through these relationships, you will discover unsuspecting ways to mutually benefit one another. But it requires you to stop pitching your idea, and start serving those around you.

CHAPTER 6.2

STOP PITCHING, START SERVING

WHEN SEARCHING FOR PARTNERS, IT'S easy to get off track trying to find the ideal partner instead of the right partner. The right partner is a person, group, or organization with overlapping needs.

For the longest time, I was envious of other towns and their community building efforts because it seemed that partners magically coalesced around good ideas. They seemed to have the perfect combination of funders, developers, politicians, and program implementers.

As hard as I tried, I could never easily get those types of partners on my side. But over the past decade, I've come to discover that partnerships don't come together as cleanly as news stories make it appear. They require persistence and patience.

Turning the co.space from a dream into a 5,000-square-foot reality taught me this firsthand.

We spent months working to line up the ideal partner. We knew we wanted to build a creative home for young changemakers. We also knew the positive impact this would have on the lives of each person who lived there as well as the broader community.

We spent countless hours applying to grant programs, pitching to fellowships and funders, and talking to foundations over the phone. When a project secures significant funding, it's more likely to be covered by the media. This makes it appear that you have to work with a big funder or fellowship for a new idea to emerge. We applied to these groups for years, assuming it was the path we had to pursue. Each time, we came out disappointed. I now look back at those denials as a badge of honor. But at the moment, they were painful reminders of how hard it was to scale our work.

We would consistently surprise our city council when we showed up to redevelopment and zoning committee meetings. We seemed to be the only young people who showed up at these inconspicuous forums. They aren't exactly your ideal way to spend a Tuesday lunch break.

We met with real estate developers and toured countless fraternities, the only buildings we could find large enough to bring our idea to life. We tried to figure out how we could satisfy a multitude of zoning ordinances that would have prevented us from turning a fraternity into anything else.

We would have explored other properties, but our town has a rule that says no more than three unrelated individuals can live together. In a college town, this prevents student housing from taking over properties that would otherwise be used for family residences, and it's an important rule to keep that balance. But it also means if you are trying to put 20 young people in a house together, the only types of properties to consider are fraternities, which have a particular zoning classification allowing them to ignore the three unrelated persons rule.

During our search, we came to discover that our town has more fraternities than nearly any other city in the world. Because of this, we have rigid zoning regulations that state if a fraternity building is sold and changes its use, it loses its legacy zoning status as a fraternity.

At first, that doesn't seem like a big deal. We weren't in the business of trying to add more fraternities to our town. But the risk came if we failed. If we bought a frat, converted it into a new cooperative housing venture, and then failed, we would be stuck with a multi-million dollar property we couldn't sell. The only people who buy giant fraternities are other fraternities (and us apparently), and we'd essentially own a fraternity building that couldn't be used as a frat.

If we wanted to get around that, we would have to get formally recognized as a fraternity. That's the last thing we wanted to pursue, but that's the path it seemed everyone in town thought we needed to follow. So we added university officials to our list of who we assumed were necessary partners.

Try as we might, we weren't able to get anywhere with our partnership building efforts. We got lots of people excited, but we could never get around the rigid rules governing our town. We created 100 different versions of our pitch deck and business plan, each tailored to various ideal partners we thought could make the whole thing work. But that's not how partnerships typically happen.

You might get lucky and land an ideal partner from, say, a cold call. But more often than not, you're going to need to find untraditional partners who share a mutual need, especially if this is your first community initiative and you don't have established partners.

While working on the co.space, we were broke. We needed a way to feed ourselves and had learned that we could pay the bills by designing posters, websites, and logos for faculty at the university. These were odd jobs that friends and colleagues handed off to us because they knew we could make things quickly versus dealing with the slow pace they were used to inside their bureaucracy.

For one of these projects, we talked with our friends in the university's Office of Global Programs. They asked us what else we were up to, as I'm sure we provided most academic offices a good bit of water cooler gossip. ("Did you see the giant blue chameleon rolling down the lawn the other day?") We told them about our pursuit to find a large house for the co.space. We vented about how frustrating the process was and how it felt like the town was making it incredibly difficult to work together to bring the dream to life. As we were leaving, they suggested we might want to contact one of their old work colleagues.

It felt like pitch No. 101. Nonetheless, I sent off a generic email that went something like: "Hi, I'm Spud. We're trying to do good things in town and want to buy a large house. Do you happen to have one?"

It may have been a little more polished than that, but not far off. I was starting to become a bit cynical about the prospects of finding something that would work, so there was no fancy pitch or explanation of what we were doing. Just the basics. It's not how

I would advise selling your idea, but I was getting tired. To our surprise, they responded to let us know they had a large house they wanted to sell. It fit what we were looking for, and it wasn't a frat.

It turns out they owned one of a handful of properties in town zoned as a boarding house, which allowed them to house multiple people without being subject to the fraternity stipulations.

In all of our time working with real estate agents, zoning officials in the borough, and experts in other communities, no one told us about boarding home zoning classifications. It felt like an answer to our prayers and such a simple solution that we had somehow overlooked.

The group that we emailed was called IFH (International Friendship House). They had been around for a few decades and managed a home for international students looking to find community. Academics primarily ran the nonprofit, and over time, the property became more than they wanted to oversee. The building needed significant renovations, and international students were finding community and housing alternatives elsewhere in town. For the past year or so, they talked internally about what to do as a board. They still wanted to provide communal living for international students, but they were also unsure how to reimagine their model.

Within 48 hours of emailing them, we had a meeting scheduled. A few days later, we were touring the property. Two weeks later, we agreed to purchase it. Six months after that, we secured the financing, signed a thick stack of papers, and had the keys in hand.

It wasn't until we stopped trying to find the ideal partners that we started to focus on what the actual need was. Partnership building requires you to identify and fill a mutual need.

We just needed a big house that accommodated 20 young people who wanted to live together. Turns out, we never actually needed a fraternity, zoning changes, university approval, or foundation funding. Without realizing it, we had been treating partnership building much like the bureaucracies we detested. We looked at the hoops around us and assumed we would have to jump through them too.

When IFH approached us with a big house and a desire to find a group willing to continue their organization's social mission, we both realized we could fill the other's needs.

One of the easiest ways to get to this point in the conversation is to ask a simple yet powerful question: How can I help you? This will reorient the conversation to explore what your potential partner needs. From there, you'll know whether or not your project can help.

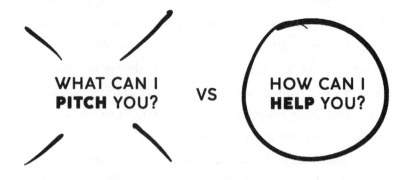

Reframing your approach to partners.

As reported by Tomas Chamorro-Premuzic in the Harvard Business Review, "a great deal of psychological research indicates that ... the key triggers of persuasion take place in the receiver of the message, whereas persuaders typically account for less than 10% of the effect." This research illustrates that there's only so much you can do (10%) to persuade someone to work with you if they are not aligned with your values or goals. By positioning yourself in a way to help your potential partner, you are finding ways to align your interests.

I love sales and getting people excited about my latest idea or vision. But never let your focus on pitching a partnership get in the way of building a relationship. Focus on people, not pitching. In building partnerships, think of your role as a party host rather than a salesperson. A great party host is always looking for people who know one another and share overlapping interests.

———————

Once we identified how we could help IFH, it was time to figure out the specifics.

We talked through lots of options. That included everything from them paying us to run the programming while they managed the leasing, to us buying the property at market value. Neither of those options worked, mainly because we didn't have that kind of money, and they didn't want to be that involved going forward.

After many weeks of ideating and trying to co-create a viable path, we landed on an agreement where they would sell the property to us for the cost of their mortgage (less than half of what the property was worth) plus a small nest egg. We signed a five-year agreement that stated if during that time frame we decided the co.space was not going to work and be able to continue its social mission, IFH would have the first right of refusal to repurchase the property at the discounted price they sold it to us. They could use the nest egg we gave them to make the necessary down payment if needed.

Once we had the deal worked out with IFH, we approached banks. Because we planned to buy the property at nearly half off, the business was cash-flow positive from Day One. My business partner and I needed cash for a down payment. After approaching our city government for support and realizing that was unlikely, we approached family members who were incredibly generous to offer us a loan.

With far more equity in the property than we were paying for it outright, nearly every bank in town made an offer. We leveraged that demand to secure a lower interest rate. The banks calculated that if we screwed up, they would get a million-dollar property for a fraction of the price.

After we purchased the property, we learned bankers were jokingly betting on how long it would take for us to screw this up. They had never sold a million-dollar property to two young, broke guys. I've always enjoyed being the underdog and having to prove others wrong.

But there was one challenge left. The bank was willing to finance the deal only if we showed we had secured a full year of leases. But we weren't allowed to advertise that we had acquired the property because we hadn't purchased it yet, and there were still people living at IFH who didn't know their home was going to be sold. We had to strike a delicate balance, which respected those currently residing at IFH, while getting 20 new tenants to sign a lease.

Here is where your early adopters save the day.

By that point, we had over 40 young people eager to join the co.space. We reached out, interviewed each of them, and selected 20 of the candidates. We asked them to sign a lease for a property they had never seen. They didn't and couldn't even know where it was located.

People on any other part of the diffusion of innovation curve would have laughed at that request. But for early adopters, who already believed in what we were doing, it just made sense to sign on the dotted line. They were so committed to the idea of building an intentional community together that they trusted Christian and me to find them the right property. They weren't worried about what amenities or utilities would be included. They just wanted in. That's the beauty of building participatory communities.

So we took our stack of 20 signed intent-to-lease documents to the bank, along with the agreement from IFH and a small down payment in the form of a loan from our families, and purchased the property. A few years later, we fully paid off the family loan and now own the property as a socially-driven for-profit.

Had we pursued the ideal partner, we would have been stuck in a messy nonprofit situation, tied to a failing Greek system in the university, with investors and steep monthly payments to make. It would never have worked.

When finding partnerships, you must always keep the mutual need at the center. What is your project's need, and how does that overlap with your potential partners' needs?

When there's alignment, developing a partnership happens rapidly and doesn't really require trying to convince anyone to partner with you. This is because your partner begins to see themselves as a creative collaborator alongside you. University of California-Davis professor Kimberly Elsbach has spent her career studying how ideas get pitched to others – from Hollywood screenwriters to new toy designers. Through her research, she's found that partners, or specifically producers that screenwriters pitch, for example, "tend to respond well if they are made to feel that they are participating in an idea's development," as she wrote in 2003 in the Harvard Business Review.

It requires a lot of persistence and a willingness to talk with as many people in your community as you can. This is the time to put all of your practice from asking probing questions to good use. Eventually, you'll stumble across the right partner, and you'll likely discover that person or organization through the networks you built with your early adopters.

Still, one challenge often remains. Despite everything else being in alignment, you may struggle to build enough trust with a partner to move forward. So what do you do if that happens?

CHAPTER 6.3

RELY ON THE COLLECTIVE TRUST OF OTHERS

ONE UNAVOIDABLE REALITY IS THAT your ideas are going to be rejected. Often, your callouts for help will frequently be dismissed. Potential partners will say no far more often than they'll say yes.

Margaret Wheatley and Deborah Frieze write about the challenge that community builders often face in "Walk Out Walk On":

> *"Pioneers have to expect to feel ignored, invisible, and lonely a good portion of the time. What they're doing is so new and different that others can't see their work even when it's staring them in the face. These are difficult dynamics to live with, especially when you know you've done good work, that you've*

solved problems that others are still struggling with. This is why it's so important that pioneers work as community, encouraging one another through the trials and risks natural to those giving birth to the new in the midst of the breakdown of the old."

Partnership building is the phase of any project that tests your commitment and persistence. Early on in my career, I was sharing an idea with a collaborator in State College. He was well-known in town as a rebellious and visionary thinker – exactly the type of person I wanted to align with. When we met, I could see in his eyes that he was excited about my idea. But he ended our time together by saying that, despite believing in my vision, he didn't have faith that I would stick around town. His experience had shown him that far too many local, young entrepreneurs had burned out in their 20s, and he didn't want to risk partnering with a group that might fizzle out a few months later.

Frustrated and determined to prove him wrong, I committed to making State College my home for the next few years. He rekindled a stubbornness in me to do what it took to earn the trust and respect of those I'd dreamed of partnering with. For nearly a decade, I persistently shared my vision for creating dynamic community spaces around town. Each time, it took on a slightly different flare depending on the year and the potential partner.

I started with New Leaf and worked tirelessly to grow and scale the space with new partners. Then through the co.space, I spent years trying to launch a "Changemaker-in-Residence" program that would recruit young creatives to live and work in our region.

Funders consistently turned down an opportunity to partner, and soon I found myself trying to launch Escape Happy Valley.

We got turned down in those partnership meetings as well. Eventually, I found myself trying to get Trailhead off the ground, which despite garnering lots of community interest, couldn't get traction.

Trailhead eventually evolved into 3 Dots and is now a proud staple of our town. But the story that rarely gets told is that this was the result of a 10-year vision I persistently championed while waiting for the right partners. During that time, the original idea would often repackage itself into new forms.

Psychology researcher Angela Lee Duckworth has dedicated much of her life to studying individuals who face challenging situations – from West Point military cadets to national spelling bee contestants. In every case, she sought to understand "who is successful and why?" Through her research, she discovered that the trait which was the most significant indicator of someone's success through challenging times was not IQ, social intelligence, or even charisma. It was grit. She notes in a 2013 TED Talk:

> "Grit is passion and perseverance for very long-term goals. Grit is having stamina. Grit is sticking with your future, day-in, day-out. Not just for the week, not just for the month, but for years. And working really hard to make that future a reality."

Forging partnerships requires a long-term view. Those I ultimately joined with to create 3 Dots shared a similar story of perseverance: They, too, had long wanted to build something that inspired a more vibrant community. We simply needed to wait until the timing was right. From my perspective, as I rallied community members together, those key partnerships began to crystalize in my living room during the Potluck Brainstorms.

On the one hand, there was the groundswell of support. We had hundreds of community members engaged in this process through monthly, informal brainstorms at my home and, eventually, with Trailhead. They were hungry to launch a gathering space for local artists and creatives, and collectively represented a loose network of arts organizations, nonprofits, and local businesses.

On the other hand, I'd wanted to partner with our community foundation to secure funding for our projects. They played a critical role as a partner to many in our community while supporting new efforts and initiatives. The foundation was responsible for distributing funds to local groups on behalf of larger national organizations like the Knight Foundation, which I'd always wanted to work with as well. But it didn't matter how much support you had from the national groups; if you didn't have the green light from the local funder, it was challenging to secure their financial investment. Despite our best efforts, however, we could never quite build enough trust with the community foundation.

But I knew they were excited to energize our downtown and amplify efforts in the arts. So we continued to make attempts and eventually invited members of their team to our Potluck Brainstorms.

While sitting in a circle around my living room – packed cozily together and trying not to spill food on one another – community members shared their desire to launch a physical space for Trailhead that would facilitate our shared vision. It seemed like everyone was excited, however with a few loose ends, the funder wasn't completely ready to financially support the vision just yet. Despite what felt like a natural overlap of needs, we couldn't seem to gain traction on securing a partnership. We had an alignment, but we hadn't yet built enough trust.

This often happens with partners, and if you find yourself in this situation, don't lose hope. Yes, it will take grit, but there are also some techniques I've found helpful when trying to partner with a group who has understandable reservations.

One of the models that has been most helpful for me is called the two loops framework. Developed by Wheatley and Frieze at the Berkana Institute, the framework explores how new ideas take root in society, and what to do when pioneers have difficulty getting people to join them on those ideas.

Loop one represents the ways things have always been done: the status quo. At some point, those systems reach a peak and begin to decline. As they go downhill, they create an incentive for others to explore a second loop – pioneers step forward to create a new system to replace the old one. They refer to these individuals as people who have walked on to explore new ways of thinking and organizing. Think of renewable energy replacing fossil fuels or Netflix replacing Blockbuster.

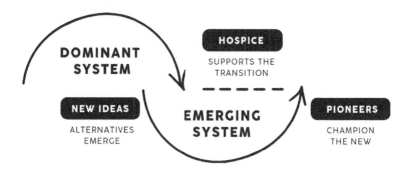

The two loops model illustrates the importance of finding ambassadors who can bring folks along into new ways of thinking.

As you might expect, it's not enough for innovations to emerge and simply replace old systems (as much as I wished that were the case). Yet that's how so many community builders tend to operate. They see the value in what they are creating and can't seem to understand why potential partners might not see it as well. But when you've been living in one loop for so long, it can be difficult to transition between the two. Pioneers and community builders often have a hard time understanding this.

The Berkana Institute refers to the critical link that helps people transition between the two loops as hospice care. Hospice is a delicate role that allows those currently maintaining the dominant system to understand and appreciate what pioneers create in the new loop. They play a vital role when pursuing new ideas, particularly in smaller communities that might be rooted in more traditional thinking. But it's not something that comes naturally to me. I'm good at breaking systems and building new ones. I live almost entirely in the second loop. As a result, I'm not great at helping people make the transition.

From the perspective of those I hoped to partner with, I represented a risk. It's only natural that individuals in the dominant system would be hesitant to partner with someone who enjoys "breaking down systems" – that's a difficult starting point in which to build trust.

At the same time, neither loop is good or bad. The new loops of today turn into old loops tomorrow. Blockbuster, at one point, pioneered something new, only to be replaced years later as they themselves became the dominant system. And regardless of which loop people live in, they play a critical role in society. Those in the first loop maintain systems and help keep a sense of stability, while those in the second loop explore emergent possibilities and alternative paths. Together, they represent the two sides of the chaordic path: chaos and order. Partnerships are critical because they find ways to bridge both sides together in healthy ways.

So I've learned over the years to rely on friends and colleagues who excel at hospice care when building partnerships. I'm great at building partnerships with fellow pioneers – folks who have already made the jump into the second loop – but I'm lousy at working with partners from the first loop. If I were going to find a way to partner with our community foundation, I knew I had to find others to serve as my intermediaries.

We were trying to create something new, and I was getting tired. Even though I had formed a tight-knit community around me, literally inviting them into my living room every month, I was on the brink of giving up trying to get a physical space launched. We had run into countless roadblocks, and I was preparing to convince our team of supporters to buy an RV instead of renting a space downtown. (I still think this is a good idea – a mobile innovation studio that can travel around your community – and perhaps one day I'll pull that off.)

At one of the Potluck Brainstorms, I started to share this frustration with a few of my early adopters. They listened with patience as I expressed my concern, and then they offered to step in and play a role. Up to this point, I was so used to trying to forge partnerships on my own that I hadn't spent enough time empowering others on my team to build the collaborations that I was unable to secure.

When you can't build trust with a critical partner, work through your early adopters who already have established that trust. Have the humility to step back and lean on others. Collaborating with others will increase your likelihood of reaching the desired partner, and allow you to keep working toward your mutual goals.

A 2014 Stanford study found that even the illusion of collaborating with others dramatically impacts your ability to persevere. In the study, individuals briefly met in a small group before being sent to separate rooms to complete a puzzle. Half of the participants were told the task was part of a much greater collaborative effort and that they would be able to share or receive tips from others. The other participants were told to work on the task alone.

Even though all of the participants worked independently, the ones who were told they were part of a larger team effort lasted 64% longer, and were less tired, more interested in the work, and achieved better results. One researcher, Gregory Walton, shared in a 2014 Stanford article that "simply feeling like you're part of a team of people working on a task makes people more motivated as they take on challenges."

Partnership building takes time and patience. Knowing that you are working towards a collective, common goal by relying on others in your community will give you the stamina you need to carry on.

Over the next few months, I spent many hours walking around my block, talking to early adopters on the phone, and mapping out strategies to convey the need we heard in the community. There was no eureka moment when it all crystalized. Even as I write this, I find myself frustrated that I can't recall a specific story to share that illustrates how to nurture these types of partnerships. But that's because they don't develop as a result of one-off moments. They happen through long walks with trusted team members, slowly working to build trust with key partners. It's not flashy, but it's important and central to the work of community building as this is often where the magic happens.

Eventually, I received a call from the funder.

It turns out they had been working on launching a downtown arts space of their own. They told me they had a property in mind. They were in discussions with the borough (who would be the landlord), and were getting ready to sign a lease with another partner in town.

But at the last minute, the partner organization that was going to sign the lease backed out. Now, they needed to find a legal entity that could sign a three-year lease on the space. There was too much risk for their organization to do so, and they needed to find a partner quickly. If they didn't, the space would go to the next person on the waitlist.

It just so happened, Trailhead was incorporated. We were one of the few groups left to partner with to ensure they didn't lose the lease to someone else.

A partnership that I had tried to form for years suddenly came together in a matter of days out of necessity. But although the need for a legal entity may have been the tipping point, the call primarily arose because our early adopters were able to convey, better than I had, the role that Trailhead might be able to play moving forward. They were able to clearly explain to the funder why a partnership was worth exploring. Your persistence pays off when your trusted relationships reach out on your behalf.

When building from the ground up, you often need to figure out how to position yourself to demonstrate your unique value. You can likely move nimbly, pivot quickly, and connect to the pulse of your town in a way that some larger organizations can't. In our case, we were able to take on the risk of signing a three-year lease. Because of that, along with the hospice care from our early adopters, Trailhead suddenly held the lease on a large space.

There were some compromises to make in terms of vision and execution. We agreed that we would rebrand, which ultimately meant Trailhead evolved into 3 Dots. But for the most part, both sides were interested in building a dynamic community space together. And collectively, we were able to achieve something far greater than if either group had ventured off on their own.

Thanks to our community foundation's support, we were guaranteed three years of "runway funding" for the project. This allowed us to sign the lease agreement, so if all else failed, at least we would have the capital required to pay rent. Without our key funding partner, we would never have been able to launch 3 Dots. And without our early adopters, we would never have found our funding partner.

Relying on ambassadors to build partnerships on your behalf is like having references when applying for a job. Your resume should show why you're qualified to do the work, but your references will vouch for why you can be trusted.

If you're unable to bridge the two loops on your own, you need to invite an intermediary along to vouch for you. Don't try to do it yourself.

———

If you find yourself staring at a blank wall trying to establish trust in a partnership and are unsure who to turn to, take some time to explore your network to unlock its social capital. We did just that with one of our early $1,000 projects we funded through the Awesome Foundation.

A local artist had wanted to paint a mural for quite some time on the side of a building in downtown State College. He had the concept sketched out, and for months had worked to gain trust and approval from various building owners, but he kept getting denied. He knew the impact the mural would have on the town and couldn't understand why it was so difficult to secure this partnership.

That's when he shared his vision with the Awesome Foundation, a group in his network that he hoped to leverage as social capital. Our trustees loved the idea and awarded him the cash. With $1,000 in his pocket, he went back to one of the building owners, and on the spot, they agreed to let him paint.

It wasn't the money that made the difference. It was the fact that he'd gotten backing for his project from a group of community members who the building owners trusted. Our project lent the artist the critical credibility he needed to bridge that gap.

The mural has since become a landmark in our community and is regularly photographed by visitors, locals, and reporters. The artist went on to paint many other murals around State College, along the main corridor to downtown and rising up to seven stories high. Had it not been for the validation that our community-funded microgrant provided, those projects may never have been approved.

The Edelman Trust Barometer is a global report that has been studying trust for over 20 years. In 2020, they found that we trust people in our community to solve challenges more than CEOs, journalists, religious leaders, or government leaders. (The only group perceived to be more trustworthy than community members was scientists.)

As you look to build trust with potential partners, consider the relationship you have with that partner and the relationship you have with others in town who might be able to lend their backing. You may not have an Awesome Foundation chapter in your community (though if you don't, you should consider launching one), but you could consider reaching out to Rotary groups, church book clubs, or even service organizations. When needed, find other networks in town who can lend their support before approaching your larger, desired partner.

———

Although partnership building comes at the end of the CANVAS framework, it's important to be nurturing relationships from Day One. After all, trusting relationships are the critical thread that runs through each of the six steps.

My favorite idea emerged as we were dumpster diving for New Leaf. But one year before we built the cardboard village, our team was focused on building relationships at our donor dinner. We knew that any crazy idea we might pursue in the coming years – like a cardboard village – would require us to have a strong network. We may not have had a robust business plan or any experience in running a nonprofit, but we knew that above all else, relationships were what mattered.

When the time came for us to host our first donor dinner, I notoriously didn't ask for money. We had organized a fancy gathering held in a barn where we'd strung up nice lights and served hors d'oeuvres to guests. We invited as many important partners as possible, including the mayor, and they all came dressed in formal attire with their checkbooks ready. Toward the end of the evening,

I got up to the mic, and everyone anticipated what was next. They were ready to hand over some cash, as partners typically do.

But we flipped the script on them. I told them I wasn't interested in their money (even though we only had a few hundred dollars in our bank account). I explained that there was no way for New Leaf to become the organization it could be if all we did was ask people to participate by writing checks. Instead, I invited them to lend us their connections, resources, media platforms, and imaginative ideas they were too afraid to try on their own. The relationships we sought to build with them as collaborators and co-creators were far more valuable than lots of cash.

From that day forward, everyone knew us as the nonprofit that held a donor dinner and didn't ask for donations. We confused a lot of old-guard leaders in town. But we rallied the local pioneers who we needed on our side. Our goal was never to find funding partners. We simply wanted to build relationships.

As a thank you that year, we sent everyone who attended light bulbs. For weeks, we meticulously sawed off the metal part of recycled light bulbs, placed rolled up, personalized thank you notes inside, and hot glued the metal connector back on. The only way to read our thank you note was to shatter the light bulb.

To pave the way for anything new, you need to be willing to smash a few ideas. Not all of your ideas will take flight or gain support from partners. To this day, there are still folks who have never broken their light bulb to see what was written on the inside. They were so used to not disrupting the status quo that they couldn't bring themselves to do it (even in the privacy of their own home).

But the ones who did smash the light bulb were hooked. These individuals would go on to be our early adopters and brand ambassadors. They regularly attended Potluck Brainstorms and joined the boards of our nonprofits. They jumped in the #BallpitofIdeas with me on our sidewalks and lent their credibility to help us secure partnerships with local government. They would often introduce us to new connections in town and were instrumental in securing large amounts of financing for many of the ventures we ran over the next 10 years.

Partnership building is nothing more than relationship building. The more you lean into the trust and support of those around you, the more you will find doors open to bring your vision to life. As those opportunities arise, all that's left to do is invite others to join you and bravely take that next step forward, together.

CONCLUSION

MAKE YOUR MARK

THE POSSIBILITY FOR CHANGE AND creativity lies at the very heart of your community, with the people who call it home. Communities change when people like you find the courage to step forward. It requires us to pick up the baton of those who have gone before us and find a way to make our mark on the community. Your voice matters when it comes to shaping the future of your town. All you have to do is get started!

In State College, I've been inspired by the overwhelming excitement of ordinary individuals who have stepped up to lead in their unique way. When my friends and I first started New Leaf, it often felt lonely and hard to find others who wanted to join us. But over time, that dynamic changes.

My favorite first follower, Cindy, won a $1,000 Awesome grant to install bird feeders outside of nursing homes during the Covid-19 pandemic. She used the money to buy a bunch of feeders and birdseed. Then she rallied community members to adopt each bird feeder so that, standing outside the windows of nursing homes, they could visit with the seniors quarantined inside. She leveraged this energy to build partnerships with many nursing homes throughout the region and generated significant local media attention for her work.

I've had friends tie-dye dozens of picnic tables just to make people smile. Others have built large structures that hammocks could be attached to so people in the community could literally hang out together. Some have converted old cigarette machines into fine art vending machines that we've placed along our sidewalks. Still, others have launched film festivals and created incubators for formerly incarcerated individuals trying to start their own businesses.

We provided funding for emerging filmmakers to make a documentary series on racial justice in our community. Others used their passion for professional pumpkin carving to raise money for an event that brought law enforcement, trauma experts, and social justice advocates together.

As each project leader has navigated how to rally support, create prototypes, and tell their story, I've watched their efforts blossom into a more creative economy. Over time, the collective contributions of numerous community members rolling up their sleeves has dramatically reshaped our region. It's created a culture where people regularly ask how they can get involved.

Research at the University of Pennsylvania has shown that a high concentration of the arts in a city leads to higher civic engagement, more social cohesion, improved child welfare, and lower poverty rates. According to a 2018 poll conducted by Americans for the

Arts, 81% of the public feels that the arts are a "positive experience in a troubled world." When we make a creative contribution, the world changes for the better.

The CANVAS framework can help you strategically approach launching an idea in your community.

While renovating the libraries in rural Pennsylvania, I stayed in a small town called Blossburg. The town has less than 1,500 people, and most people driving through would never stop except to get gas. Yet, it's in towns like these where I have come to discover some of my favorite creative community builders.

We so often look to big cities for inspiration. We tell ourselves that innovation trickles down from urban areas into rural regions. But I've come to appreciate that frequently the reverse is true. The overlooked and sometimes underappreciated areas of a country have some of the richest lessons to teach us.

Chris Harris of the Kauffman Foundation, one of the most prolific funders of entrepreneurship ecosystems in the U.S., highlighted this insight in a 2020 article on the organization's website:

> "Innovation, diversity of ideas and people, and new concepts don't need to be imported to rural communities – they're already there. Rural entrepreneurs and community leaders have always, by necessity, been innovative. Rather than defining rural communities by the progress that is believed to have stopped, we can instead choose to define them by the progress they've made despite massive disinvestment and, perhaps, by the progress they could make if they had the support."

The Oasis game was born out of the favelas, low-income settlements, in Brazil. Organizations like Thrive are actively reimagining communities in the deep south when others might overlook them, not waiting for approval from the cities. And it's here in Blossburg where I came to meet a few of my favorite collaborators.

Jill and Shane Nickerson grew up in Blossburg and have been there most of their lives. Neither originally had aspirations of getting involved in local government or necessarily leading their community.

As Jill shared with me early on, "I wanted to make a positive change in our community, but I didn't know how." Growing up, Shane preferred to spend his time skateboarding. But he was often scolded and kicked around by others in the community. Unlike football or basketball, skateboarding wasn't seen as a legitimate pastime in town. Leaders in the area assumed skateboarders simply caused trouble. But life has a funny way of throwing us curve balls. Today, Shane is known as the "Skateboarding Mayor" of Blossburg.

In their story, you can see precisely how the CANVAS framework applies to creating meaningful change in a community.

Step 1: Chart Your Path
The journey that led the Nickersons to this point started in the early 2000s when they began charting a path for what their community might look like. They would regularly hang out in the parts of town where kids would build skateboarding ramps and transform everyday structures into edges they could grind down.

The more time they spent with kids, the more inspired they

DESIGNING CREATIVE COMMUNITIES

were by their creativity and how they saw the community around them. A bench was no longer simply a bench. It was something they could try and jump over as part of a grand trick.

Step 2: Ask Probing Questions
Over the years, the Nickersons noticed that their region was experiencing a significant brain drain, yet nothing was being done to engage the youth. These kids had so much creativity to contribute to the town, and yet they were never included in conversations around economic development. At worst, they were written off as destructive to the area.

But Jill and Shane weren't afraid to hang out in the fringes of their community, building up social capital with anyone committed to making their town a better place. They asked probing questions and started to identify a real need they could address: forming a dedicated skatepark in Blossburg.

Step 3: Name Early Adopters
Energized by the idea, Jill found some state funding for the project. Then she made her pitch to the borough council to see if they would partner with her to make it happen. Despite her excitement and preparation, her pitch was denied. Those in power didn't see the value of the project and wrote it off.

Devastated, Jill came home and decided that evening she would run for borough council. If she couldn't find a way to partner with them, she would simply join them. So instead of assembling partners as she initially hoped, she started to name early adopters. A few loyal first followers helped her run for borough council, and her idea gained momentum.

Step 4: Visualize a Prototype

With the proposed skatepark facing more roadblocks than anticipated, the Nickersons realized they needed to help their community see things differently. They had to inspire their community to be active participants in creating change. So they started to paint the town.

I like to think of communities as a canvas, but Jill and Shane applied the metaphor quite literally. They got a truck, bought some paint, and started repainting buildings in their downtown. They started with their own building to show what was possible and, eventually, found a Main Street development grant to cover the cost of supplies. Over time, they managed to convince many of the other downtown business owners – regardless of how hesitant or initially stubborn they were – to repaint their buildings. Blossburg was becoming their literal canvas and they began to visualize a prototype of what it would take to get their community involved.

Step 5: Articulate Your Story

During this time, Jill, with her first followers' help, made it onto borough council. They were ready to make their skatepark pitch for a second time.

They now had the momentum from early adopters and had learned how to articulate their story to gain support. They explained why a skatepark would be beneficial to the area. And they added that the ramps could simply be rolled off if all else failed, and basketball hoops installed instead. Skeptical city leadership softened, and the skatepark got the greenlight.

They gathered a few kids in the community and built a prototype of what the park could look like out of poster boards.

The kids cut out various ramps and half-pipes as they designed their ideal skatepark, and when the time was ready, they helped build the park themselves.

The Nickersons had learned the value of telling a compelling story and proactively reached out to their media contacts to ensure the project quickly gained credibility.

Step 6: Sustain Efforts with Partners

Although initially skeptical, the community and borough council saw the impact the skatepark was having. Excited to now have this in their community, they wanted to support more creative efforts.

To sustain their efforts with partners, they created a group called Blossburg VIBE (Visions in Business and Entertainment). Jill and Shane helped spearhead the effort with the goal to launch community projects that enhanced the quality of life for those who live, work, play, or attend school in the area. They set up a simple Facebook page and told anyone in their community they could drop in on their regular meetings to share an idea. All were welcome to partner.

Soon, they were supporting everything from hosting fall festivals to organizing holiday light contests. Jill often took the role of identifying creative ways to energize the community, while Shane found the resources to make them happen.

Shane went on to become the mayor of Blossburg. Not exactly the career choice he initially saw for himself, he decided to approach the position untraditionally.

The Nickersons were aware that many families in the community had limited resources, and the kids would often share skateboards at the park. So when Shane heard of a skate shop in a nearby town going out of business, he decided to buy all the skateboards. He made it his personal mission to offer a free skateboard to any kid in town that didn't have one. He spent his Saturdays at the skatepark and proceeded to let any kid pick out a board of their own to keep.

The skatepark continued to get more attention and draw more skaters. Soon, the Nickersons were running out of skateboards to hand out. So Jill and Shane pursued the next logical step: They bought a press machine online to design and produce their own decks for skateboards. One thing led to another, and they eventually teamed up with a pro skater, Ron Allen, to launch Mayor Skateboard Company. That allowed them to produce limited-run decks manufactured in Blossburg while amplifying the story of what was happening in their town.

Successful community efforts emerge when trust is given out as freely as Jill and Shane gave out skateboards. It is the most critical currency you can leverage as a community builder. This requires that you spend time in the fringes of your community, working face-to-face with the people you serve. Many local government officials wouldn't consider skateboarders to be ideal collaborators, but Shane and Jill weren't constrained by such stereotypes or preconceived notions. They're the kind of city leaders who would have happily jumped into the dumpster with me to collect cardboard.

Having not grown up with the bias of what innovation should look like or how to behave as a mayor, my friends in Blossburg paved their own path. When they took on leadership positions, they didn't try to fit into a mold of what a community leader should look like.

They charted a path forward that was unique to them and their style. Creative community building is much like skateboarding. In the same way a skater can reimagine everyday structures to create DIY skateparks, community builders start by looking at what's available to them. That includes their contacts, resources, time, and creativity. They leverage those relationships and assets to reimagine what might be possible for their town.

Today, Shane and Jill have dreams of converting an old warehouse they bought into an indoor skatepark and alternative school built around skateboarding. With their empty warehouse – overflowing with rundown lumber and scrap metal – they have teamed up with the superintendent who championed renovating the school's libraries into innovation centers.

They are working with the art department to paint a giant mural on the outside of the building that says "Community." One day they could imagine using the space to teach kids how to design and market skateboards, understand the physics and mathematics behind their favorite tricks, and help them get comfortable speaking in public to share their work.

On the building's second floor, they are designing creative living spaces along with a coworking space and coffee shop for the community, all with views that look down on the indoor half-pipe below. Collectively, the project brings together the four pillars of a creative community: live, work, learn, and play. The project isn't complete – as they are just starting to chart their path for what the idea might become – but that's how every idea begins. It starts with the courage to pursue a curiosity and see where it might lead.

When we first started working together, they told me they were tired of the perception that their kids had to wait for innovation to trickle down from big cities. They wanted to disrupt that narrative and show their community they could use their region's unique assets to be creative in their own way.

Seeing what's happening in Blossburg reinforces that communities don't need to wait on the cities or the experts to tell them how to innovate. They simply need to start adding to their own canvas.

As your idea grows and evolves, you will find others excited to step up and lead in their own way. It is in these moments that communities begin to change. A single idea can inspire 10 more. What you do can spur others to become more proactive, to contribute their gifts, and be participants in the changes they wish to see as well. All that's required, as the prominent psychologist Carl Rogers wisely notes, is for you to believe, "What I am is good enough if I would only be it openly."

Don't listen to those who say you shouldn't hand out skateboards for free. Don't listen to those who scoff at your plans to dumpster dive for cardboard. If you have a creative idea for how to make your community a better place, pursue it. Chart your path, build prototypes, rally friends, and take your first steps to contribute to your community. As Brené Brown writes:

> "At the end of the day, at the end of the week, at the end of my life, I want to be able to say that I contributed more than I criticized."

So how will you elevate the place where you live? How will you contribute to the unfolding story of your community? Dust off your courage and relentlessly follow your curiosity to go make your mark.

ABOUT THE AUTHOR

Spud Marshall is a serial social entrepreneur, creative community builder, and lover of fog machines. He is the founder of My Creative Community, which supports groups in designing engaging experiences for their communities. He serves as a facilitator, coach, and consultant alongside organizations ranging from the Sullivan Foundation, Nasdaq Entrepreneurial Center, and Pennsylvania Council on the Arts to Teach for America, the American Planning Association, and Johnson & Johnson.

In addition to his community consultation work, he founded 3 Dots Downtown, a community arts and innovation event center, where he served as the Innovation Director. He is also the founder and chief catalyst for the co.space, a 20-person intentional community for young changemakers, which has been listed as one of the top disruptive innovations to emerge in higher education. Prior to those efforts, Spud founded New Leaf Initiative, which currently serves as a dedicated co-working space and innovation incubator.

He has been honored as a Knight Foundation Emerging Cities Champion, listed as one of the top millennial civic leaders in the country, and been featured as one of the "Foremost Under 40" Business Leaders in central Pennsylvania. Spud has a Masters in Strategic Sustainability Leadership and a pretty spectacular failure resume (reach out if you're interested). He currently resides in State College, Pennsylvania with his wife, loyal dog, and curious cat.

To view his most recent projects and to explore ways to partner with Spud, visit www.mycreative.community. You can also reach him by emailing spud@mycreative.community.

ACKNOWLEDGEMENTS

People aren't lying when they say writing a book is a labor of love. The only difference between the long hours writing versus those spent building cardboard furniture at New Leaf, painting large swaths of white walls at 3 Dots, and building cave showers at the co.space, was that my dog got to cuddle closely on the couch beside me as I typed. His companionship was constant. For all the running around my projects typically entail, I'm sure he appreciated the fact that this project was a largely reflective and sedentary one. For anyone who knows me, you are well aware that Bodi is attached at my hip on every venture I tackle.

Throughout the past year of writing, I have found myself in constant admiration of all those who invest equally long hours and share a steadfast belief about what's possible in their communities. For the creatives who often go unseen in your community, you've been on my mind throughout this entire journey. And for everyone providing encouragement and love, please know that your role in supporting those spearheading creative initiatives is invaluable. You ensure that those of us who see the world differently and invite others to step into that new reality don't simply stand out as a "lone nut."

To Katie, my unbelievably supportive wife, thank you. Thank you for reminding me that I should eat every now and then, and that my worth is never found in the ventures I start. Thank you for listening to early audio versions of my first drafts read in a computer-generated robot voice because you much prefer audiobooks over reading. You patiently listened as I shared my thoughts on the latest chapters while we played long games of Settlers most nights. Ever since our first date geeking out about the diffusion of innovation, you have inspired me to lead with authenticity and humility. I count myself forever blessed to be journeying through life alongside you.

To Michael, I couldn't have asked for a better editor. Thanks for your brilliance in being able to streamline my early thoughts and providing accountability to help me finish this project. I'm so thankful that Lara introduced us! To Tori, thanks for your amazing design support in putting this book together. To Adam, thanks for catching all of the tiny grammar errors. To Chad, thanks for turning me on to Pink Sheets, which became an invaluable tool for organizing my ideas and packaging this book. And thanks for officiating my wedding (can't say thank you enough for that)!

To the countless co-conspirators and creative troublemakers I've had the honor to work with so far, thank you for all your insights and the late nights spent working on a website until the sun began to rise, and the long chats around a bonfire dreaming up ways to better the world around us. I feel humbled knowing there are so many of you – from the amazing team in Southern Tioga School District and Blossburg to all those who have attended an Ignite Retreat.

To Christian, thanks for sending me an email years ago telling me you had a few million dollars to start our dream company and asking if I would move back to the states to start it with you. We never could have imagined the journey that unfolded. Despite the fact that there was never any cash as you'd hoped (a story for another time), I'm beyond grateful for the path it led us down. There's no one else who would have put in as much time as you had for no pay or promise of what might emerge. Thanks for dreaming alongside me and hustling to make that dream a reality – not just for the two of us, but for the town we called home. And thanks for fixing our hacked website when I was at JPL (I still owe you for that one).

To Eric, thanks for agreeing with a handshake in your driveway when we were in high school to build a better world together. You saw what was possible for this town long before many others came around to that vision and deserve a lot of credit for that. Thanks for your friendship and patience as we all explored what it would take to make New Leaf a reality. I appreciate you generously paying rent for those first few years, and also that you didn't question it when we turned your recumbent bike into a giant chameleon.

To everyone else who was involved in New Leaf in those early days, thank you. Countless interns jumped in, with little guidance, to help build the organization. You filed our taxes, dug up grass in fields to create outdoor offices on our sidewalk, and went door-to-door collecting pianos for us. None of our successes would be possible without each of you putting in those long hours.

Thanks to those who joined me for the Educate 20/20 road trip and co-created one heck of an adventure. Thanks to all of the local leaders and entrepreneurs who rallied behind us and lent your validation – you know who you are. And most importantly, thanks to Cindy for being the best landlord I have ever had.

To every co.spacer – from short-term tenants to house managers – thanks for stepping up to show our town what intentional communities are all about. There is magic that happens within those walls that few will understand unless they have lived there. Thanks for the courage you have all shown to lead with vulnerability and boldness (and for putting up with the occasional bees who escape into the home). And a massive thanks to the IFH leadership team for believing in a few young guys and giving us a chance when few others would.

To the entire 3 Dots team, thanks for helping me bring to life a vision I held for so many years. The overwhelming response we've had from the community is all because of your partnership and commitment. To the board, few see how much time you put in behind the scenes to make this organization financially feasible. To Harvey, thanks for stepping up at a time when we were all trying to figure out what 3 Dots would become. That was no easy feat to juggle (and I'm glad you had Winston at your side through much of it; as did Bodi)!

To every trustee who has donated over the years – thank you! You were our early adopters who fearlessly got behind 3 Dots before any of us knew what it would become. Also, to those trustees who have been with us from the very beginning when we were starting up Trailhead, I see you!

To my family, thanks for encouraging me to pursue alternative career paths, even when they were confusing to understand. Thanks for your generosity with your time and resources – from volunteering the Educate 20/20 RV and then peeling off the stickers we plastered to the vehicle, to donating spare kitchen cabinets for the co.space and ripping up the old carpet we threw out the third floor windows. You have shaped who I am today and instilled in me the creativity and drive to breathe life into mere ideas.

Lastly, I want to acknowledge the privilege I have with this work. I look back on my journey and am quite mindful of the opportunities I was given because I have a supportive family and am a straight, white male. I've put in long hours to champion a vision for my community, but I've also had fewer hoops to jump through than many minoritized community builders.

As we are confronted with the racial and social injustices that are prevalent throughout society, I am hopeful that change is possible. But we still have a long way to go. I encourage you to seek out and support the work of those tackling injustice in their own communities. To every person reading this book – who I am beyond thankful for for joining me and bearing witness to the stories shared – if there is any way I can support or amplify the work you are doing in your community, please reach out.

Communities are built hand-in-hand with those you love. So to all of you who have joined me over the years – offering your caring support, willingness to collaborate, and encouragement to one day write a book – this one's for you!

TIMELINE

2004
APRIL   Build (and accidentally destroy) a parade float

2007
MAY   Visit with Paradise in Tanzania

2010
JUNE   Visit Oasis Game in the Netherlands
AUGUST   New Leaf launched
OCTOBER   New Leaf flooded

2011
APRIL   New Leaf re-launched (for a second time after flood)
JUNE   Visit Ashoka offices in D.C.
JULY   Pianos placed on sidewalks – and promptly removed
SEPTEMBER   Move into Cindy's basement

2012
JANUARY   Adopt Pascal the chameleon
FEBRUARY   Educate 20/20 Road trip
     co.space "What If?" video sent to online competition
APRIL   Host New Leaf donor dinner
JULY   Win online competition for co.space video
AUGUST   Approach IFH about partnering on the co.space
     Build and ride around in a blue chameleon car
NOVEMBER   Win GeeBiz competition for the co.space
DECEMBER   Host the co.space prototype cabin retreat

2013
MARCH   Purchase the co.space
APRIL   Host the New Leaf cardboard village party
     Host the co.space Mentor Meetup prototype
AUGUST   First tenants move into the co.space
SEPTEMBER   Attend the NASA Jet Propulsion Lab event

2014

FEBRUARY	New Leaf launched in the borough building
AUGUST	Start a Bubbleball soccer company
OCTOBER	Rebel Alliance secret society started

2015

FEBRUARY	Attempt to launch "Changemaker-in-Residence"
MAY	Indoor beehive installed at the co.space
JUNE	Bees escape from indoor beehive at the co.space

2016

SEPTEMBER	Regret starting a Bubbleball soccer company
DECEMBER	Escape Happy Valley idea launched

2017

MAY	Test cardboard innovation trailhead prototype
NOVEMBER	Visit with the rubber-band prototype in Boulder, Co.

2018

JANUARY	Host first Potluck Brainstorm
FEBRUARY	Begin recruiting Trailhead first followers
MARCH	Establish State College Awesome Foundation chapter
MAY	Coordinate Library Innovation Lab renovations
	First $1,000 Awesome Grant awarded
JUNE	Launch Trailhead organization
	Host wedding reception
JULY	Begin ELF bike marketing plan

2019

JANUARY	3 Dots launched
	Host 3 Dots community design charrettes
MAY	Furniture store shopping spree
JUNE	Harry Potter-esque picture frame wall built
AUGUST	Build the Mothership and host pop-up sidewalk party
SEPTEMBER	Lounge in the #BallpitofIdeas on the sidewalk

NOTES

Introduction: Designing Creative Communities

1. Inga Vitols, "Americans Believe the Arts Strengthen Communities Socially, Educationally, Economically" September 27, 2018, https://www.americansforthearts.org/news-room/press-releases/americans-speak-out-about-the-arts-in-new-public-opinion-poll

2. "Facts & Figures on the Creative Economy" https://nasaa-arts.org/nasaa_research/facts-figures-on-the-creative-economy/

3. Frank Newport, "Americans Big on Idea of Living in the Country" December 7, 2018, https://news.gallup.com/poll/245249/americans-big-idea-living-country.aspx

4. Bernard Darras, "Creativity and Creative Communities" August 14, 2018, https://doi.org/10.1002/9781118978061.ead099

5. Marie Haaland, "New Research Shows Young Americans Are Optimistic About Creating Change" November 19, 2019, https://www.swnsdigital.com/2019/11/majority-of-young-americans-think-theyre-doing-more-to-change-the-world-than-older-generations/

6. Anne Kniggendorf, "Making a small town home" December 5, 2019, https://www.kauffman.org/currents/making-a-small-town-home/

7. The Policy Circle, "The Creative Economy" https://www.thepolicycircle.org/minibrief/the-creative-economy/

8. Jason Duff, "Millennial Innovators Are About to Leave Big Cities" December 21, 2016, https://fortune.com/2016/12/21/millennials-cities/

Step 1: Chart Your Path

1. James Kouzes and Barry Posner, "To Lead, Create a Shared Vision" January 2009, https://hbr.org/2009/01/to-lead-create-a-shared-vision

2. Linda Kay Klein, Rebecca Kauffman, and Scott Sherman, "Work on Purpose Curriculum" October 15, 2013

3. Peter Flade, Jim Asplund, and Gwen Elliot, "Employees Who Use Their Strengths Outperform Those Who Don't" October 8, 2015, https://www.gallup.com/workplace/236561/employees-strengths-outperform-don.aspx

4. Brian Brim, "How a Focus on People's Strengths Increases Their Work Engagement" May 2, 2019, https://www.gallup.com/workplace/242096/

focus-people-strengths-increases-work-engagement.aspx

5. Maria Popova, "Fixed vs. Growth: The Two Basic Mindsets That Shape Our Lives" January 29, 2014, https://www.brainpickings.org/2014/01/29/carol-dweck-mindset/

6. Paul O'Keefe and Carol Dweck, "Implicit Theories of Interest: Finding Your Passion or Developing It?" October 29, 2018, https://www.ncbi.nlm.nih.gov/pmc/articles/PMC6180666/

7. Melissa Witte, "Instead of 'Finding your passion,' try developing it, Stanford scholars say" June 18, 2018, https://news.stanford.edu/press-releases/2018/06/18/find-passion-may-bad-advice/

8. Abigail Abrams, "Yes, Impostor Syndrome Is Real. Here's How to Deal With It" June 20, 2018, https://time.com/5312483/how-to-deal-with-impostor-syndrome/

STEP 2: ASK PROBING QUESTIONS

1. Leslie Davis and Kim Parker, "A half-century after 'Mister Rogers' debut, 5 facts about neighbors in U.S." August 15, 2019, https://www.pewresearch.org/fact-tank/2019/08/15/facts-about-neighbors-in-u-s/

2. Vanessa K. Bohns, "A Face-to-Face Request Is 34 Times More Successful Than an Email" April 11, 2017, https://hbr.org/2017/04/a-face-to-face-request-is-34-times-more-successful-than-an-email

3. Melissa Dahl, "A Third of Americans Have Never Met Their Neighbors" August 24, 2015, https://www.thecut.com/2015/08/third-of-americans-dont-know-their-neighbors.html

4. Meaghan McDonough, "We don't know our neighbors anymore. Here's what that costs us." October 10, 2017, https://www.bostonglobe.com/magazine/2017/10/10/don-know-our-neighbors-anymore-here-what-that-costs/m9sTUVbmi3XFfxRN96Ft9M/story.html

5. Kim Parker, Juliana Menasce Horowitz, Anna Brown, Richard Fry, D'Vera Cohn, and Ruth Igielnik, "How urban, suburban and rural residents interact with their neighbors" May 22, 2018, https://www.pewresearch.org/social-trends/2018/05/22/how-urban-suburban-and-rural-residents-interact-with-their-neighbors/

6. George Gao, "Americans divided on how much they trust their neighbors" April 13, 2016, https://www.pewresearch.org/fact-tank/2016/04/13/americans-divided-on-how-much-they-trust-their-neighbors/

7. Kaveh Sadeghian, "How to Use Design Thinking for Personal Growth + Social Innovation // Ignite Masterclass" November 23, 2020, https://youtu.be/TbpakxbC5Uc

8. "The Top 20 Reasons Startups Fail" November 6, 2019, https://www.cbinsights.com/research/startup-failure-reasons-top/

9. Phil Santoro, "Why Startups Fail | Lessons From 150 Founders" February 8, 2021, https://www.wilburlabs.com/blueprints/why-startups-fail

10. Chad Littlefield, "We! Connect Cards" https://weand.me/product/we-connect-cards/

11. Peter Himmelman, "How Thinking Like a Kid Can Spur Creativity" October 13, 2016, https://time.com/4529444/how-thinking-like-a-kid-can-spur-creativity

12. Francesca Gino, "The Business Case for Curiosity" September - October 2018, https://hbr.org/2018/09/the-business-case-for-curiosity

13. Rohini Venkatraman, "You're 96 Percent Less Creative Than You Were as a Child. Here's How to Reverse That" January 18, 2018, https://www.inc.com/rohini-venkatraman/4-ways-to-get-back-creativity-you-had-as-a-kid.html

14. George Land, "The Failure Of Success" February 16, 2011, https://www.youtube.com/watch?v=ZfKMq-rYtnc&feature=youtu.be&t=5m29s

15. Jeanne Liedtka, "Why Design Thinking Works" September - October 2018, https://hbr.org/2018/09/why-design-thinking-works

16. Mike Fishbein, "The Ultimate List of Customer Development Questions" https://mfishbein.com/the-ultimate-list-of-customer-development-questions/

STEP 3: NAME EARLY ADOPTERS

1. Derek Sivers, "How to start a movement" February 2010, https://www.ted.com/talks/derek_sivers_how_to_start_a_movement

2. Nancy Lee and Philip Kotler, "Social Marketing: Behavior Change for Social Good" 2019, https://us.sagepub.com/en-us/nam/social-marketing/book260584

3. International Social Marketing Association (iSMA), "What is Social Marketing? How Does it Differ from Communications and Policy? | ft. Nancy Lee" May 16, 2018, https://youtu.be/aQ-LGRFXZoo

4. Les Robinson, "A Summary of Diffusion of Innovations" January 2009,

https://twut.nd.edu/PDF/Summary_Diffusion_Theory.pdf

5. Rebecca Dahl, Larysa Metanchuk, and Steve Marshall, "Engaging Action: A Systemic Approach to Communication Design of Social Marketing Campaigns for Behaviour Adoption" 2010, https://www.diva-portal.org/smash/get/diva2:831532/FULLTEXT01.pdf

6. Laura Methot, "How to Deal With 'CAVE People' — Citizens Against Virtually Everything" Spring 2019, https://www.rotman.utoronto.ca/Connect/Rotman-MAG/IdeaExchange/Spring2019-Methot

7. Carrie Jones, "Creating a Community Commitment Curve" https://www.carriemelissajones.com/blog/community-commitment-curve

8. Jon Davidson, "What's Working in Cities: CreateHere in Chattanooga" July 27, 2011, https://www.secondwavemedia.com/concentrate/features/createhere0158.aspx

9. "Stand for State impact" https://studentaffairs.psu.edu/campus-community-diversity/stand-state/about-stand-state

10. Junko Sasaki and Ken Royal, "Engaged Followership: The Foundation of Successful Leaders" July 12, 2019, https://www.gallup.com/workplace/260561/engaged-followership-foundation-successful-leaders.aspx

11. Brian Brim, "Strengths-Based Leadership: The 4 Things Followers Need" October 9, 2015, https://www.gallup.com/cliftonstrengths/en/251003/strengths-based-leadership-things-followers-need.aspx

12. "5 Quick Tips for Engaging "Interested Bystanders" in Local Government" August 15, 2015, https://medium.com/community-pulse/5-quick-tips-for-engaging-interested-bystanders-in-local-government-5ea4d56d8d

13. Lee Rainie, Scott Keeter, and Andrew Perrin, "Trust and Distrust in America" July 22, 2019, https://www.pewresearch.org/politics/2019/07/22/trust-and-distrust-in-america/

14. Diane Gavarkavich, Angelique Gaines, LaTonya Williams, and Leslie Gutierrez, "Charting the Civic Landscape: The Interested Bystander, in Charlotte Context" November 30, 2018, https://knightfoundation.org/reports/charting-the-civic-landscape-the-interested-bystander-in-charlotte-context/

15. "Digital Formats are Among the Most Trusted Advertising Sources Despite Slow Growth" September 28, 2015, https://www.nielsen.com/us/en/insights/article/2015/digital-formats-are-among-the-most-trusted-advertising-sources-despite-slow-growth/

16. "Under the Influence: Consumer Trust in Advertising" September 17,

2013, https://www.nielsen.com/us/en/insights/article/2013/under-the-influence-consumer-trust-in-advertising/

17. Kate Krontiris, John Webb, and Chris Chapman, "Understanding America's Interested Bystander: A Complicated Relationship with Civic Duty" 2015, https://research.google/pubs/pub44180/

18. Kevin Vallier, "Why Are Americans So Distrustful of Each Other?" December 17. 2020, https://www.wsj.com/articles/why-are-americans-so-distrustful-of-each-other-11608217988

19. Scott Sherman, "Transformative Action Institute Teacher's Manual" 2013, https://www.transformativeaction.org/

STEP 4: VISUALIZE A PROTOTYPE

1. Tim Merry, "Steps to navigate change" April 30, 2014, https://www.findtheoutside.com/blog/2014/4/30/steps-to-navigate-change

2. Kim Parker, Juliana Menasce Horowitz, Anna Brown, Richard Fry, D'Vera Cohn, and Ruth Igielnik, "Americans' satisfaction with and attachment to their communities" May 22, 2018, https://www.pewresearch.org/social-trends/2018/05/22/americans-satisfaction-with-and-attachment-to-their-communities/

3. "Oasis Game" https://www.emotiveprogram.org/project/oasis-game/

4. Ann Markusen and Anne Gadwa, "Creative Placemaking" 2010, https://www.arts.gov/about/publications/creative-placemaking

5. "Breaking Down Creative Placemaking" April 19, 2016, https://kresge.org/resource/breaking-down-creative-placemaking/

6. Katherine Loflin, "Learning From Knight's Soul of the Community, Leaning Toward the Future of Placemaking" April 10, 2013, https://www.pps.org/article/learning-from-knights-soul-of-the-community-leaning-toward-the-future-of-placemaking

7. "Knight Soul of the Community" 2010, https://knightfoundation.org/sotc/

8. Mike Lydon, Dan Bartman, Tony Garcia, Russ Preston, and Ronald Woudstra, "Tactical Urbanism: Volume 2" 2012, http://tacticalurbanismguide.com/guides/tactical-urbanism-volume-2/

9. Keith Stuart, "Hello Lamp Post and the idea of playful cities" June 27, 2013, https://www.theguardian.com/technology/gamesblog/2013/jun/27/hello-lamp-post-playful-cities

10. Mark McNielly, "The Creativity Gap" May 10, 2012, https://www.fastcompany.com/1836840/creativity-gap

11. Chip Heath and Dan Heath, "The Power of Moments: Why Certain Experiences Have Extraordinary Impact" 2017, https://heathbrothers.com/the-power-of-moments/

12. Katharine Schwab, "Ideo Studied Innovation In 100+ Companies—Here's What It Found" March 20, 2017, https://www.fastcompany.com/3069069/ideo-studied-innovation-in-100-companies-heres-what-it-found

13. Jacob Nelson, Tobias Mahan, Christopher McComb, and Jessica Menold, "The Prototyping Behaviors of Startups: Exploring the Relationship Between Prototyping Behaviors and Startup Strategies" March 2020, https://asmedigitalcollection.asme.org/mechanicaldesign/article-abstract/142/3/031107/1069610/The-Prototyping-Behaviors-of-Startups-Exploring?redirectedFrom=fulltext

14. Benedict Sheppard, Hugo Sarrazin, Garen Kouyoumjian, and Fabricio Dore, "The business value of design" October 25, 2018, https://www.mckinsey.com/business-functions/mckinsey-design/our-insights/the-business-value-of-design

15. "The Lighter, Quicker, Cheaper Transformation of Public Spaces" https://www.pps.org/article/lighter-quicker-cheaper

STEP 5: ARTICULATE YOUR STORY

1. Donald Miller, "Building a Story Brand" 2017, https://buildingastorybrand.com/

2. Kate Harrison, "A Good Presentation Is About Data And Story" January 20, 2015, https://www.forbes.com/sites/kateharrison/2015/01/20/a-good-presentation-is-about-data-and-story

3. Carmine Gallo, "Stories literally put our brain waves in sync" June 6, 2018, https://qz.com/work/1298571/stories-literally-put-our-brain-waves-in-sync/

4. Kent Hendricks, "The peak-end rule" October 7, 2019, https://kenthendricks.com/peak-end-rule/

5. Leo Wildrich, "The Science of Storytelling: Why Telling a Story is the Most Powerful Way to Activate Our Brains" December 5, 2012, https://lifehacker.com/the-science-of-storytelling-why-telling-a-story-is-the-5965703

6. Jeremy Hsu, "The Secrets of Storytelling: Why We Love a Good Yarn" August 2008, https://www.scientificamerican.com/article/the-secrets-of-storytelling/

7. Cell Press, "How curiosity changes the brain to enhance learning" October 2, 2014, https://www.sciencedaily.com/releases/2014/10/141002123631.htm

8. Matthias Gruber, Bernard Gelman, and Charan Ranganath, "States of Curiosity Modulate Hippocampus-Dependent Learning via the Dopaminergic Circuit" October 2, 2014, https://www.cell.com/neuron/fulltext/S0896-6273(14)00804-6

9. Ian Sample, "Curiosity improves memory by tapping into the brain's reward system" October 2, 2014, https://www.theguardian.com/science/2014/oct/02/curiosity-memory-brain-reward-system-dopamine

10. "'Who shared it?': How Americans decide what news to trust on social media" March 20, 2017, https://www.americanpressinstitute.org/publications/reports/survey-research/trust-social-media/

11. Joanne Fritz, "9 Ways to Get the Local Media Interested in Your Nonprofit Story" November 20, 2019, https://www.thebalancesmb.com/tips-local-media-relations-2502364

12. Jesse Singal, "Fake News Spreads Because People Trust Their Friends Too Much" March 21, 2017, https://nymag.com/intelligencer/2017/03/fake-news-spreads-because-people-trust-their-friends-too-much.html

13. Cyril Bouquet, Jean-Louis Barsoux, and Michael Wade, "Bring Your Breakthrough Ideas to Life" November - December, 2018, https://hbr.org/2018/11/bring-your-breakthrough-ideas-to-life

14. "How journalists find their news, use social media and work with PR teams in 2020" March 12, 2020, https://muckrack.com/blog/2020/03/12/state-of-journalism-2020

STEP 6: SUSTAIN EFFORTS WITH PARTNERS

1. Joyce Hoelting, "Building trust in communities" 2017, https://extension.umn.edu/vital-connections/building-trust-communities

2. Ruth De Backer and Eileen Kelly Rinaudo, "Improving the management of complex business partnerships" March 21, 2019, https://www.mckinsey.com/business-functions/strategy-and-corporate-finance/our-insights/improving-the-management-of-complex-business-partnerships#

3. Kimberly Elsbach, "How to Pitch a Brilliant Idea" September 2003, https://hbr.org/2003/09/how-to-pitch-a-brilliant-idea

4. Tomas Chamorro-Premuzic, "Persuasion Depends Mostly on the Audience" June 2, 2015, https://hbr.org/2015/06/persuasion-depends-mostly-on-the-audience

5. "2020 Edelman Barometer of Trust" January 19, 2020, https://www.edelman.com/trust/2020-trust-barometer

6. Clifton Parker, "Stanford research shows that working together boosts motivation" September 15, 2014, https://news.stanford.edu/news/2014/september/motivation-walton-carr-091514.html

7. Angela Lee Duckworth, "Grit: The power of persuasion and perseverance" April 2013 https://www.ted.com/talks/angela_lee_duckworth_grit_the_power_of_passion_and_perseverance

8. Kelsie Anderson and Aubrey Francisco, "The Research Behind the TED Talk: Angela Duckworth on Grit" March 6, 2019, https://digitalpromise.org/2019/03/06/research-behind-ted-talk-angela-duckworth-grit/

1. Deborah Frieze, "Two Loops: How Systems Change" December 16, 2010, https://vimeo.com/17907928

Conclusion: Make Your Mark

1. Randy Cohen, "10 Reasons to Support the Arts in 2020" March 23, 2020, https://blog.americansforthearts.org/2020/03/23/10-reasons-to-support-the-arts-in-2020

2. Inga Vitols, "Americans Believe the Arts Strengthen Communities Socially, Educationally, Economically" September 27, 2018, https://www.americansforthearts.org/news-room/press-releases/americans-speak-out-about-the-arts-in-new-public-opinion-poll

3. Chris Harris, "After generations of disinvestment, rural America might be the most innovative place in the U.S." December 14, 2020, https://www.kauffman.org/currents/rural-america-most-innovative-place-in-united-states/

Made in United States
North Haven, CT
17 May 2024

52582047R00214